THE PUKA GUIDE

100 Hawaiian-Style Hole-in-the-Wall Restaurants

Laura...
See you in line!
- John -

Eat with your eyes!
Dmax

THE PUKA GUIDE

100 Hawaiian-Style
Hole-in-the-Wall
Restaurants

Donovan M. Dela Cruz
Jodi Endo Chai

WATERMARK
PUBLISHING

ISBN 978-0-9790647-2-2

Library of Congress Control Number: 2007929068

Design
Leo Gonzalez

Production
Maggie Fujino

Cover art by Kelly Sueda, whose oil paintings are available at
locations throughout Hawaii.

Watermark Publishing
1088 Bishop St., Suite 310
Honolulu, Hawaii 96813
TELEPHONE 1-808-587-7766
TOLL-FREE 1-866-900-BOOK
EMAIL sales@bookshawaii.net
WEB SITE www.bookshawaii.net

Printed in the United States

puka (poo-kah) *n.* hole, opening,
a hole in the wall ...

Dedicated to the restaurant owners, managers and workers who helped make this guidebook possible. Mahalo for all you do to keep Hawaii's local-style dining traditions alive.

CONTENTS

ACKNOWLEDGMENTS

Special mahalo to Chef Alan Wong, artist Kelly Sueda, designer Leo Gonzalez and to George Engebretson, Duane Kurisu, Aimee Harris, Maggie Fujino, Nicole Chew and Dawn Sakamoto of Watermark Publishing.

Thank you also to our families. For Donovan: Larry Dela Cruz, Pat Dela Cruz and Donalyn Dela Cruz. For Jodi: Garrett, Jenna and Ethan Chai; Harry and Nancy Endo; Aaron and Cathy Okinaka and family; and David and Serena Chai.

And mahalo to Lance Tomasu, Kim and Ken Kobayashi, Dana Harvey, Shan Tsutsui, Laura Figueira, Kim Ribellia, Kyle Chock, Kacy Sumikawa, Jennifer Soriano, Lee and Janel Yoshimura, Craig and Joy Fujikawa, Wade and Cindy Matsumoto, Barry and Denice Inciong, Joni Taba, Sharon Suzuki, Vincent Itoga, Shawn Ching, Ken and Jan Fukada, Cathy Cruz and Kathy Muneno.

FOREWORD
by Chef Alan Wong

When I was a teenager, my friends and I found jobs working for the Dole pineapple plantation. After a hard day in the fields of central Oahu, we'd grab a bite to eat at a hole-in-the-wall in Wahiawa. This little eatery was like my second home: the waitresses all knew me and the food was as close as anyone could come to my mom's delicious home cooking.

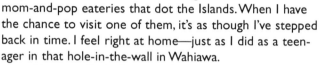

Even now, after a long day in my restaurant kitchens, I still hunger for the simple foods served at the charming mom-and-pop eateries that dot the Islands. When I have the chance to visit one of them, it's as though I've stepped back in time. I feel right at home—just as I did as a teenager in that hole-in-the-wall in Wahiawa.

Donovan Dela Cruz and Jodi Endo Chai have captured a bit of Old Hawaii—and an important part of Island culture—in *The Puka Guide*. You never know what hidden culinary treasures you'll find at these off-the-beaten-path eateries.

But first, of course, you have to find them. And that's where this book comes in. It's a journey I always look forward to taking!

INTRODUCTION

Steaming hot manapua. Chewy chichi dango. Crispy, crunchy potato chips. Flaky manju. Buttery shortbread cookies.

Hawaii is in love with food; our local culture is centered around it. Where we go to find our Island treats—restaurants, bakeries, cafés, drive-ins, saimin stands, okazuya and omiyage shops—varies as much as the food itself. And some of the most popular spots are no more than pukas, or holes, in the wall.

There are hundreds of these holes-in-the-wall throughout the Islands, so narrowing the field wasn't an easy task. We knew that the food needed to be unique to Hawaii—not something you'd ordinarily or easily find in, say, Omaha or Green Bay. Also, we wanted places with a nostalgic feel—be it furnishings or food—that would remind us of small-kid time. Lastly, we chose businesses that do little or no advertising.

This new edition of *The Puka Guide* is a completely updated compilation of our three previously published hole-in-the-wall guides: *The Okazu Guide* and *The Puka Guide* and *The Omiyage Guide*. We've revisited the "pukas" in those earlier books and added new ones from Hilo to Hanapepe.

WHAT IS A "HOLE IN THE WALL"?

A hole-in-the-wall restaurant is just what you'd imagine. It's usually an eatery that's nestled in a row of storefronts or tucked away in a little shopping center off the beaten path, in a place you'd least expect it. In some cases, if you blink you'll miss it!

These are the places that you only hear about by word-of-mouth. Sometimes they barely have available parking, much less a place to sit.

They don't serve anything fancy—no trendy cuisine that's "infused" or "caramelized." They serve comfort food, home cooking just like Mom used to make. The food brings you back to the good old days: having dinner with the family at a local coffee shop, eating a teri burger with fries and a shake at the drive-in after school, or enjoying a steaming hot bowl of saimin with the gang after a high school football game.

Many of these businesses are family-owned, passed down from generation to generation. Some of the owners launched their restaurants just because they enjoyed cooking so much. Others started their places as grocery stores, then expanded to serve prepared dishes.

Regardless of how these little eateries came to be, we're delighted that they're still around. And though they may be small in size, they're a big part of our lives—and of today's Island culture.

OKAZUYA & OMIYAGE

A large part of the local hole-in-the-wall culture are the okazuya and omiyage shops.

Before Hawaiian Regional Cuisine, before fast food—even before the plate lunch—there was okazu, the unique blend of dishes and delicacies that helps define the Hawaii experience.

You find the best okazu at the okazuya, usually a little eatery tucked away in a weathered building or a modest shopping center. Technically, the word is a combination of the Japanese *okazu*, side dish, and *ya*, shop. But in the Islands, the okazuya is much more than just a Japanese food shop. A true product of Hawaii's cultural melting pot, it has roots in the Islands' multi-ethnic plantation culture. We visited okazuya that serve up a real chop-suey mix of local delicacies, such as teri fried chicken, Spam-stuffed eggplant and sweet potato crumble. Okazu is a simple, even nostalgic, Island institution that keeps alive the spirit of a slower, simpler bygone era.

Some of these shops have carved out quite a reputation for themselves. So much so that when we visit Neighbor Islands, we go out of our way to pick up some treats for family and friends—we call it omiyage. Omiyage

is a Japanese word meaning "souvenir gift." The Japanese travel tradition of bringing back gifts for family and friends has become an important part of Hawaii's culture.

Omiyage can really be anything—toys, jewelry, craft-work—but it's best when it's food. Many holes-in-the-wall and okazuya shops prepackage their most popular items and have devised special travel boxes that will survive a plane ride to a Neighbor Island or back to the Mainland. Some shops specialize in only omiyage. From cakes, candies and cookies to artisan breads and vacuumed-packed, marinated meat, the shops offer unique gift ideas.

In choosing omiyage, it's important to remember that it's not the cost of the gift but, more important, the brand, its uniqueness and, of course, its taste. Sometimes it's not even what you give, but where you got it. It's also important to note that presentation isn't necessarily a priority. While a plain white box won't excite anyone, their mouths will certainly water when they discover the tasty treats inside. But most important, of course, is this: it really is the thought that counts. So, to prevent any last-minute airport omiyage shopping, we marked the places that specialize in omiyage with a gift box icon.

USING THIS BOOK

This is a workbook as much as it is a guidebook. We've provided room for you to jot down notes on your favorite items, a secret parking spot, the best time to go or the cost of the pre-packed bento. Use it to help hone your skills and become a true puka hunter!

It was our aim to sample as much of Hawaii's great food as we could, then share the locations and specialties with our readers. You'll notice that the shops and restaurants in this book run the gamut from the famous and familiar to the low-key and off-the-beaten-track. The rest are somewhere in between. But no matter which ones you visit, when you taste what they have to offer, we guarantee you'll keep coming back for more.

And don't forget: always buy extra omiyage, because you never know who you might forget.

FIND AND GRIND!

We wrote this book for friends and family who love to eat and for people like us who won't settle for anything but the real thing. We also wrote it for those who are new to the Islands and have only heard or read about these hole-in-the-wall food meccas. This book will give you the inside scoop on all your favorite puka eateries and introduce you to some you never knew existed. The guide includes locations statewide, so get started and eat your way across Hawaii! Take along some wet-wipes and get messy! Taste everything and, above all, have fun!

We know that there are "pukas" we still haven't discovered, so if you stumble across one, be sure to make a note of it. Then use the coconut wireless and spread the word.

Happy hunting!
Donovan M. Dela Cruz
Jodi Endo Chai

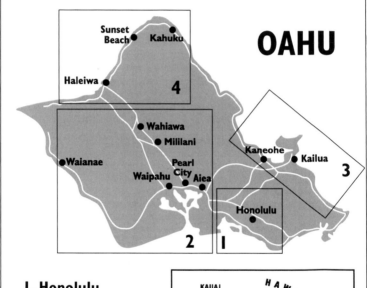

OAHU

Sunset Beach • Kahuku

Haleiwa •

4

• Wahiawa

• Mililani

Kaneohe • • Kailua

• Waianae

Waipahu • Pearl City • Aiea

3

• Honolulu

2 **1**

1. Honolulu
2. Central/Leeward
3. Windward
4. North Shore

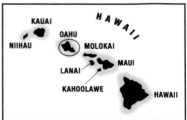

KAUAI

NIIHAU

H A W A I I

OAHU

MOLOKAI

LANAI

MAUI

KAHOOLAWE

HAWAII

OAHU

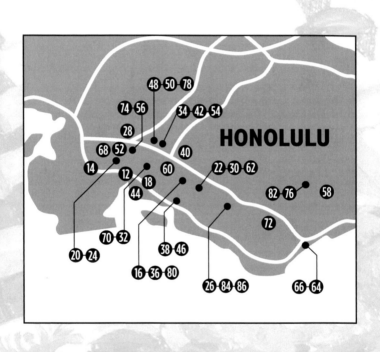

HONOLULU

"The secret is in the dashi. It has always been made from scratch with fresh ingredients and never powdered soup base. The serious saimin eaters will always notice that. Today, there are just a handful of original saimin stands that make their saimin the old-fashioned way—we're proud to be known as one of them!"

Toshiaki Tanaka

Boulevard Saimin

WHERE STAY?	1425 Dillingham Boulevard Honolulu, Hawaii 96817 Phone 841-7233 (on the ewa-makai corner of Dillingham Boulevard and Waiakamilo Road)
WHEN OPEN?	Monday - Saturday, 9:30 a.m. - 9 p.m. Sunday, 9:30 a.m. - 4 p.m.
GOTTA GRIND	Saimin (their dashi soup is homemade), inari sushi, shrimp tempura, barbecue stick, homemade hamburger sandwich or hamburger steak with brown gravy
SEATING	Make house! (27 tables)
PARKING	Happy hunting! (small parking lot and street parking)
INSIDE SCOOPS	Closed Labor Day, Thanksgiving, Christmas Day, New Year's Day
CATERING?	No
ESTABLISHED	1956 (at this location since 1960)
NOTES	

"Since we're close to the airport and right behind the Plaza Hotel, we meet a lot of people, especially tourists. Most of the time, we're like directory assistance—we're always telling them how to get places or where to go!"

Marian Wong

Byron's Drive-In

WHERE STAY?
3297 North Nimitz Highway
Honolulu, Hawaii 96819
Phone 836-0541
(near the airport, behind Plaza Hotel)

WHEN OPEN?
Open all day, every day

GOTTA GRIND
Shrimp burger, "yellow" or "red" sauce burgers, teriyaki beef, hamburger steak, beef stew, beef curry, oxtail soup, oxtail stew

SEATING
Make house! (seats 87)

PARKING
No sweat! (large parking lot)

INSIDE SCOOPS
Breakfast is served all day. Company checks accepted.

CATERING?
Yes

ESTABLISHED
1965

NOTES

"*I never saw myself doing this, but I love what I do and cooking food the way we like to eat it. Positive comments about what we offer really keep us going.*"

Sharlene Koga

Caryn's Okazuya

WHERE STAY? 1270 Young Street, # 1
Honolulu, Hawaii 96814
Phone 597-8083
(look for the Japanese banner "nobori" on
the pole in front)

WHEN OPEN? Wednesday - Saturday, 6 a.m. - 2 p.m.
Monday, Tuesday & Sunday, closed

GOTTA GRIND Okazu: Inari sushi, mochiko chicken, teri
mahi, eggplant/Spam tempura

SEATING Keep your eyes open! (4 tables, but
sometimes they fill up fast!)

PARKING No sweat! (large parking lot)

CATERING? Yes

ESTABLISHED 1940s (Sharlene Koga took over the
business in 1985. Caryn's has been in this
location since 1990.)

NOTES

"*Our pork products are made in public view, and we use first-grade lean pork—so lean that some of our competitors say we're using corned beef instead of pork!*"

Harry Y.N. Mau

Char Hung Sut

WHERE STAY?	64 North Pauahi Street Honolulu, Hawaii 96817 Phone 538-3335
WHEN OPEN?	Monday, 5:30 a.m. - 2 p.m. Tuesday, closed Wednesday - Sunday, 5:30 a.m. - 2 p.m.
GOTTA GIVE	Char siu manapua, pork hash, ma tai su
BESIDES OMIYAGE	Chow fun, dim sum
SEATING	Take-out only!
PARKING	No sweat! (street parking and parking lot)
INSIDE SCOOPS	For early morning orders, it is best to order your items the day before; closed for vacation during September and October. Cash only.
CATERING?	No
ESTABLISHED	1945
NOTES	

"My father started the noodle business in 1942. I took over in 1987 and added the manapua and retail food business. I don't personally cook the food, but I seem to have a knack for knowing what people want. Lesson No. 1: Think like the customer. None of us in the family had any significant prior food retailing experience. But with some luck, we have been very successful. It just amazes us that we have come this far, and we expect to go further."

Nelson Chun

Chun Wah Kam
Noodle Factory

WHERE STAY? 505 Kalihi Street
Honolulu, Hawaii 96819
Phone 485-1107

WHEN OPEN? Kalihi:
Monday - Friday, 6:30 a.m. - 4 p.m.
Saturday, 6:30 a.m. - 4:30 p.m.
Sunday, 7 a.m. - noon

Waimalu:
Monday - Tuesday, 8 a.m. - 4:30 p.m.
Wednesday - Saturday, 8 a.m. - 8:30 p.m.
Sunday, 8 a.m. - 4 p.m.

GOTTA GIVE More than a dozen varieties of
manapua, including kalua pig and garlic
chicken flavors

BESIDES OMIYAGE Retail and wholesale noodle products,
Chinese lunch and dinner plates

SEATING Kalihi: Take-out only!
Waimalu: Make house (20 tables,
42 chairs)

PARKING Kalihi: Keep your eyes open! (6 stalls)
Waimalu: No sweat! (Waimalu Shopping
Center parking lot)

INSIDE SCOOPS Ordering in advance is not required.
Both stores are open 364 days of the year.
No personal checks, but credit cards
accepted.

CATERING? Yes

ESTABLISHED 1942

NOTES _____

_____

_____

*"It feels like we bring
back a sense of nostalgia.
We still use brown
paper wrap. We like to
remember how it
used to be."*

Colleen Kuromoto

Ebisu Catering Service

WHERE STAY? 1915 South King Street
Honolulu, Hawaii 96826
Phone 941-6055
(between Pumehana and McCully Streets,
across from Honolulu Craft Supply)

WHEN OPEN? Monday - Tuesday, 7 a.m. - 2:30 p.m.
Wednesday, closed
Thursday - Saturday, 7 a.m. - 2:30 p.m.
Sundays & Holidays, 7 a.m. - 2 p.m.

GOTTA GRIND Okazu: Maki sushi, inari sushi, chow fun,
teri chicken, nishime

BESIDES OKAZU Okinawan sweet potato pie

SEATING Take-out only! (We suggest you enjoy
your okazu at nearby Old Stadium Park!)

PARKING Good luck! (street parking in front
of the shop)

INSIDE SCOOPS Closed each year Jan. 1-7.

CATERING? Yes

ESTABLISHED 1962

NOTES _____

_____

_____

_____

_____

_____

_____

_____

_____

_____

_____

"*I moved from Japan to Hawaii more than 30 years ago. I didn't know where to work; I didn't speak any English, so cooking was all I could do, since you no need to speak to customers. Now my husband is the one who cooks, and I do everything else. I enjoy what I do—even my customers have become my friends.*"
Ethel Ishii

Ethel's Grill

WHERE STAY?   232 Kalihi Street
Honolulu, Hawaii 96819
Phone 847-6467
(Kalihi industrial area, corner of
Kahai and Kalihi Streets)

WHEN OPEN?   Monday - Saturday, 6 a.m. - 2 p.m.
Sunday, closed

GOTTA GRIND   Okazu: Tataki sashimi in Ethel's secret
sauce, cold ginger chicken, lau lau plate,
Japanese-style hamburger steak

SEATING   Make house! (7 tables)

PARKING   Happy hunting! (limited parking under
the building, street parking)

INSIDE SCOOPS   Very crowded from 11 a.m. - 2 p.m.,
so get there early!

CATERING?   Yes, on Sundays only.

ESTABLISHED   1976

NOTES

_____

_____

_____

_____

_____

_____

_____

_____

_____

_____

"My great-grandfather
started this business, then
my grandfather ran it,
then my mom and dad.
Now, my wife and
I are taking over."

Arrison Iwahiro

Fukuya Delicatessen & Catering

WHERE STAY?	2710 South King Street Honolulu, Hawaii 96826 Phone 946-2073 (a few doors up King Street from Puck's Alley)
WHEN OPEN?	Monday - Tuesday, closed Wednesday - Sunday, 6 a.m. - 2 p.m.
GOTTA GRIND	Okazu: Sushi, chow fun, fried chicken, teri ahi, mochiko chicken, miso butterfish, sea burger, croquettes, BBQ/hotdog/ chicken rolls (great for a meal-on-the-go or a day on the golf course), tofu dishes
BESIDES OKAZU	Mochi and cookies (order the cookies in advance because they sell out fast)
SEATING	Keep your eyes open! (one table and a long bench outside)
PARKING	Happy hunting! (6 stalls in front of the building and street parking—metered stalls, only during certain hours)
INSIDE SCOOPS	Closes for a two-week annual vacation in early March. For purchases more than $10, they accept personal checks and credit cards.
CATERING?	Yes
ESTABLISHED	1941 (opened by current owners' great- grandparents; at this location since 1979)
NOTES	

Gulick Delicatessen

WHERE STAY?	1512 Gulick Avenue Honolulu, Hawaii 96817 Phone 847-1461 Fax 848-0391 (where you'd least expect it—in the middle of a Kalihi residential area; nearest cross street is North School.)
WHEN OPEN?	Monday-Saturday, 8 a.m. - 4 p.m. Sunday, 8 a.m. - 2 p.m.
NEW LOCATION	1936 South King Street Honolulu, Hawaii 96826 Phone 941-2835 Monday - Friday, 7 a.m. - 4 p.m. Saturday - Sunday, 10 a.m. - 4 pm.
GOTTA GRIND	Hash patty (sized for 2 people—it's huge), shoyu butterfish, California roll, and anything fried (tempura, chicken—don't know how they keep it so crispy!)
BESIDES OKAZU	Some Filipino and Chinese dishes
SEATING	Take-out only! (suggest you enjoy your food at nearby Moanalua Gardens or Kalihi Park)
PARKING	Happy hunting! (street parking only)
INSIDE SCOOPS	Especially during lunch hour, it gets crowded so be sure to remember to take a number. It also helps to have your order in mind. Accepts credit cards.
CATERING?	Yes
ESTABLISHED	1970
NOTES	_____ _____ _____

"We place high value on freshness and healthy foods, and our food has an authentic Japanese taste."

Tom Jones

Gyotaku

WHERE STAY? 1824 South King Street
Honolulu, Hawaii 96826
Phone 949-4584
Fax 946-6529
(Mauka side of King Street between
Punahou and McCully Streets)

WHEN OPEN? Okazuya:
Daily, 9 a.m. - 2 p.m. (Take-out orders
available until restaurant closes.)
Restaurant:
Sunday - Thursday, 11 a.m. - 9 p.m.
Friday - Saturday, 11 a.m. - 10 p.m.

GOTTA GRIND Okazu: Sushi, broiled butterfish, salmon
and saba, tempura, teri, mochiko and
karaage chicken, short ribs

BESIDES OKAZU Sushi and pupu platters, assortment
of bentos. For large orders: "Okazu-By-
The-Pan" (fried noodles, Chinese chicken
salad, fruit salads)

SEATING Take-out only!

PARKING No sweat! (large parking lot with
about 50 stalls)

INSIDE SCOOPS Gyotaku's famous shoyu-vinaigrette
dressing is available here. This is their
second restaurant. The first is in Pearl
City (formerly Kyotaru Restaurant) at
98-1226 Kaahumanu Street; 487-0091.
Credit cards accepted.

CATERING? A party room at the restaurant seats
up to 30.

ESTABLISHED 2002 (replacing Suehiro, here since 1975)

OKAZU TRIVIA Co-owner Tom Jones trained as a sushi
chef in Japan, owns Gyotaku with
Willy Okimoto and Tony Sato.

"In the late 90s, I started cooking and seasoning Okinawan sweet potatoes in a small deep fryer in my own apartment kitchen. The growing demand from my friends, co-workers and family led me to create a company to manufacture these gourmet potato chips."

James "Jimmy" Chan

Hawaiian Chip Company

WHERE STAY?   717 North King Street
(near Tamashiro Fish Market)
Honolulu, Hawaii 96817
Phone 845-9868

WHEN OPEN?   Monday - Friday, 6:30 a.m. - 5 p.m.
Saturday, 9 a.m. - 3:30 p.m.
Sunday, closed

GOTTA GRIND   The Original Flavor Taro Chip is cooked
to perfection and lightly salted, making
a scrumptious snack with lots of taste
and texture. The Zesty Garlic Flavor Taro
or Sweet Potato Chips offer a mouth-
watering blend of garlic, onion, salt and
jalapeno. The Kilauea Fire is the company's
hottest chip. The spicy blend of habanero,
cayenne pepper, onion, garlic, and salt will
make your taste buds sizzle.

SEATING   A small booth area

PARKING   No sweat! Parking right out front

INSIDE SCOOPS   Beyond its King Street location, you
can find Hawaiian Chips at Wholesale
Unlimited and several other locations.
Call 845-9868 to find the location
nearest you. You can also pick up large-
size bags at all three Costco locations on
Oahu. King Street location accepts credit
cards and personal checks with local I.D.

CATERING?   No, but custom orders are available

ESTABLISHED   January 2000

NOTES   _____

_____

_____

_____

"At one time, my sisters-in-law and I managed two dress shops and the restaurant. Now I'm semi-retired and spend most of my time in the dress shop. I'm not ready to retire yet—I'm still enjoying it!"

Jane Nakasone

Jane's Fountain

WHERE STAY?	1719 Liliha Street Honolulu, Hawaii 96817 Phone 533-1238 (next to L&L Drive-Inn on the Diamond Head side of the street)
WHEN OPEN?	Monday - Friday, 6 a.m. - 10 p.m. Saturday - Sunday, 7 a.m. - 2 p.m.
GOTTA GRIND	Saimin, sandwiches, plate lunches
SEATING	Make house! (8 booths)
PARKING	Happy hunting! (metered street parking)
INSIDE SCOOPS	Closed for one week around New Year's.
CATERING?	No
ESTABLISHED	1937 (at current location since 1948)
PUKA TRIVIA	In 1984, Jane Nakasone took over the restaurant from her father-in-law. By coincidence, it was already named Jane's Fountain for her sister-in-law.
NOTES	

"Friendly and experienced employees coupled with unprecedented recipes and elegant packaging makes Kapuakea Products a best kept secret located within the heart of Hawaii's capital"

Sharon Toriki

Kapuakea
products
439 Kamani Street

Kapuakea Products

WHERE STAY?   439 Kamani Street
Honolulu, Hawaii 96813
Phone 596-7855

WHEN OPEN?   Monday - Thursday, 9 a.m. - 5 p.m.
Friday, 9 a.m. - 1 p.m.
Saturday - Sunday, closed

GOTTA GIVE   Lilikoi lemon bars, banana poi bread
(This is a "preorder" bakery–baking only
what is ordered; at least two working
days' notice is required.)

BESIDES OMIYAGE   Gift baskets and specialty gifts (Hawaiian
jams, preserves, tea sets and Hawaiian
grilling sauces

SEATING   Take-out only!

PARKING   No sweat! (2 parking spaces in front,
sometimes a few spaces in the
adjacent lot)

INSIDE SCOOPS   Ordering two days in advance is always
required, as Kapuakea only bakes what is
ordered. They require more notice if it's a
large order or during the holidays. They
start taking Christmas orders from
November 1st. Items are perishable and
should be refrigerated within 2-3 days.
Closed the first week of January. Accepts
personal checks and credit cards.

CATERING?   No, but they do platters

ESTABLISHED   1988

NOTES   _____

_____

_____

_____

"We've helped people start their businesses in the past and then my husband encouraged me to open my own. I love it— there are no regrets."

Karen Yamaoka

Karen's Kitchen

WHERE STAY?
614 Cooke Street
Honolulu, Hawaii 96813
(in the two-story building between
Queen and Halekauwila Streets)
Phone 597-8195

WHEN OPEN?
Monday - Friday, 5:30 a.m. - 9 p.m.
Saturday, 5:30 a.m. - 3 p.m.
Sunday, closed

GOTTA GRIND
Pulehu ribs, Hawaiian plate (comes with
lau lau, choice of kalua cabbage or chicken
long rice, opihi, ahi poke, dessert, rice,
salad and homemade Portuguese sausage)

SEATING
Make house! (15 tables)

PARKING
Keep your eyes open!
(small parking lot, plus street parking)

INSIDE SCOOPS
Closed Thanksgiving, Christmas Day,
New Year's Day. Karen's also can host
private parties. Accepts company checks
and travelers cheques.

CATERING?
Yes, (Karen's Catering, 983-4186)

ESTABLISHED
1993

NOTES

"The love of chocolate got me started in the business! I studied chocolate-making in Hong Kong. People are always happy to get chocolates. We get to create them, and it allows us to meet all kinds of people."

Wendy Loh

Kona Paradise Candies

WHERE STAY? 128 South School Street
Honolulu, Hawaii 96813
Phone 599-8777

WHEN OPEN? Monday - Friday, 8 a.m. - 5 p.m.
Saturday - Sunday, by appointment only

GOTTA GIVE Chocolate-covered fortune cookies with personalized messages inside, boutique chocolates, chocolate oreos and more!

SEATING Take-out only!

PARKING No sweat! (4 parking stalls in front of the building)

INSIDE SCOOPS To allow time to pack, advance orders are preferred. The company also offers healthy options: they are Hawaii's Juice Plus distributor. Cash and personal checks accepted.

CATERING? No

ESTABLISHED 1989

NOTES

_____

_____

_____

_____

_____

_____

_____

_____

_____

_____

_____

"The business remains a Takakuwa family-owned business. Recipes and methodologies are passed on from one generation to the next by key personnel. Fortunately for us, we have wonderful longtime employees who continue to perfect the status quo and teach those at the next level. Good people, high ethics and morals, and consistency make a solid formula to longevity."

Dion Yasui

Liliha Bakery

WHERE STAY? 515 North Kuakini Street
Honolulu, Hawaii 96817
Phone 531-1651

WHEN OPEN? Monday, closed
From 6 a.m. Tuesday - Saturday,
open 24 hours
Sunday, 6 a.m. - 8 p.m.

GOTTA GIVE Coco puffs, an pan, chantilly cakes,
custard pies, pancake mix, frozen waffles

BESIDES OMIYAGE Liliha Bakery's coffee shop serves "cooked
before your eyes" hot meals at the
counter.

SEATING Keep your eyes open! (18 stools for
coffee shop patrons only)

PARKING No sweat! (parking lot)

INSIDE SCOOPS Customers don't need to call in advance.
If you're taking items on the airplane,
they recommend you keep the items in
a cool place; most products require
refrigeration. Closed at the beginning
of each year for about a week. Accepts
personal checks.

CATERING? No

ESTABLISHED 1950

NOTES
_____

_____

_____

_____

_____

_____

_____

"*What we've learned is that it's important for family to support and encourage one another. It hasn't been easy, but we're thankful to the Lord for guiding us to where we are now.*"

Lester and Irene Yonamine

Lox of Bagels

WHERE STAY?   111 Sand Island Access Road
Honolulu, Hawaii 96819
Phone 845-2855

WHEN OPEN?   Monday - Friday, 5 a.m. - 3 p.m.
Saturday, 6 a.m. - 2 p.m.
Sunday, closed

GOTTA GIVE   Bagels, bagel chips (cinnamon sugar,
butter/garlic, parmesan), bagel puffs

BESIDES OMIYAGE   Bagel sandwiches, espresso drinks,
soup/salad bagel platters

SEATING   Keep your eyes open! (5 small tables)

PARKING   No sweat! (parking lot)

INSIDE SCOOPS   When traveling off-island, bagel chips
need to be hand-carried. To ensure you
get what you want, they recommend you
place your order in advance. No personal
checks. Accepts credit cards.

CATERING?   No

ESTABLISHED   1997

NOTES   _____

_____

_____

_____

_____

_____

_____

_____

_____

_____

"We enjoy the freedom of doing what we want to do, and watching the business grow."

Burt Fujii and Faith Kimura

Makiki Bake Shop

WHERE STAY? 1302 Young Street
Honolulu, Hawaii 96814
Phone 596-7366

WHEN OPEN? Monday - Friday, 6 a.m. - 2 p.m.
Saturday, 6 a.m. - noon
Sunday, closed

GOTTA GIVE Biscuits and orange chiffon cake

SEATING Take out only!

PARKING Keep your eyes open! (limited parking)

INSIDE SCOOPS For large orders or for travel off-island,
call in advance to place an order.
Makiki Bake Shop closes when the food
runs out. Accept personal checks with
proper ID.

BESIDES OMIYAGE Assorted pastries and cakes

CATERING? No

ESTABLISHED The bakery opened more than 20 years
ago. In 1997, Burt Fujii and Faith Kimura
acquired the business from the original
owners.

NOTES

"*We're still here because of luck and a lot of hard work. I always count my blessings.*"

Lyle Nonaka

Mitsu-Ken Okazu & Catering

WHERE STAY? 1223 North School Street
Honolulu, Hawaii 96817
Phone 848-5573
Fax 848-5521

WHEN OPEN? Monday - Saturday, 4:30 a.m. - 1 p.m.
Sunday, closed

GOTTA GRIND Okazu: Garlic chicken, shrimp tempura,
chicken yakitori stick, sweet potato
tempura

BESIDES OKAZU Assorted bento, plate lunch specials
(stuffed cabbage, turkey, etc.), and their
breakfast special (fried rice and egg
— and inexpensive, too!)

SEATING Keep your eyes open! (2 outdoor tables)

PARKING Happy hunting! (2 parking stalls next to
the okazuya and street parking; don't
park on the street 6:30 a.m. - 8:30 a.m. or
you'll get a ticket.)

INSIDE SCOOPS Although they don't close when the food
runs out, be sure to get there early for
the best selection!

CATERING? Yes

ESTABLISHED 1993

OKAZUYA TRIVIA Mitsu-Ken is owned by Lyle Nonaka and
Brad Kaneshiro

NOTES _____

_____

_____

_____

_____

"*I love the freedom to create new items for our customers.*"

Daryll Nakama

Mitsuba Delicatessen

WHERE STAY? 1218 North School Street
Honolulu, Hawaii 96817
Phone 841-3864
(Just look for the sign standing in the
parking lot — it features a musubi
cartoon character.)

WHEN OPEN? Monday - Saturday, 5 a.m. - 1 p.m.
Sunday, closed

GOTTA GRIND Okazu: Hot dog musubi, fried chicken,
butterfish, Okinawan sweet potato
crumble

BESIDES OKAZU Breakfast food, plate lunch and the
Nanakuli—a larger version of the
loco moco

SEATING Take-out only!

PARKING Good luck! (parking lot fills up fast)

INSIDE SCOOPS Food usually runs out before closing,
so get there early for the best selection.

CATERING? Yes

ESTABLISHED 1983

NOTES

"My staff does an excellent job so I can spend a lot of time building boats and fishing!"

Thomas Mukaigawa

Monarch Seafoods

WHERE STAY?
515 Kalihi Street
Honolulu, Hawaii 96819
Phone 841-7877
(corner of Kalihi and Colburn Street)

WHEN OPEN?
Lunch: Monday-Saturday, 10 a.m. - 2 p.m.
Sunday, closed

Store Hours
Monday-Thursday, 9 a.m. - 5 p.m.
Friday, 9 a.m. - 6 p.m.
Saturday, 9 a.m. - 3 p.m.
Sunday, closed

GOTTA GRIND
Nori-wrapped, crab meat-stuffed ahi;
Bento Number 1 (crab cakes, mochiko
chicken, fried poke); lemon-peppered
broiled salmon

SEATING
Take-out only!

PARKING
Happy hunting! (street parking only)

INSIDE SCOOPS
Closed on major holidays;
personal checks accepted with Hawaii I.D.

CATERING?
Yes

ESTABLISHED
1996

NOTES
_____

_____

_____

_____

_____

_____

_____

_____

_____

_____

"*People compare our place to 'Cheers,' because it's where everybody knows each others' names. The customers are like family—they even bus the tables for us! They're so nice. Our restaurant feels like it's one big family kitchen.*"

Shirley Higa

New Uptown Fountain

WHERE STAY?   522 North School Street
Honolulu, Hawaii 96817
Phone 537-1881
(near the corner of School and
Liliha Streets)

WHEN OPEN?   Monday - Saturday, 6:15 a.m. - 12:45 p.m.
and 5 p.m. - 7 p.m.
Sunday, 7 a.m. - 12:45 p.m.

GOTTA GRIND   "Tachi" has two hamburger steaks,
3 scrambled eggs, rice and salad.
"Magee" is large saimin with vegetables
and wun tun

SEATING   Keep your eyes open! (5 booths and
4 tables)

PARKING   Happy hunting! (5 stalls, street parking
on School Street)

INSIDE SCOOPS   New Uptown Fountain can get crowded,
but the turnaround is quick.

CATERING?   No

ESTABLISHED   1940s

PUKA TRIVIA   Owners Tom and Shirley Higa took over
the business from their uncle in 1983.
They want people to know more about
the Okinawan language, which is why they
gave their dishes Okinawan names.

NOTES   _____

_____

_____

_____

_____

_____

KINGYOKU
75¢

UGUISU MOCHI
70¢

HABUTAI MOCHI
50¢

TSUMAMI MOCHI
50¢

PEANUT BUTTER

"This has been a family business from the beginning. We work at providing a quality product at the best price. It's protein and a lot of carbs. A lot of people like the fact that there are no preservatives."

Mike Hirao

Nisshodo Candy Store

WHERE STAY?   1095 Dillingham Boulevard, Building I-5
Honolulu, Hawaii 96817
Phone 847-1244

WHEN OPEN?   Monday - Friday, 7 a.m. - 4 p.m.
Saturday, 7 a.m. - 3 p.m.
Sunday, closed

GOTTA GIVE   Chichi dango, peanut butter mochi,
habutai mochi

SEATING   Take-out only!

PARKING   Happy hunting! (small parking lot)

INSIDE SCOOPS   Order at least two days ahead. Accepts
personal checks.

CATERING?   No

ESTABLISHED   1918 (at this location since 1986)

NOTES   _____

_____

_____

_____

_____

_____

_____

_____

_____

_____

_____

_____

_____

_____

"We serve local plate lunches made with care. Come in and experience the difference."

Wayne Takushi

North Shore Grinds

WHERE STAY?   1429 10th Avenue
Honolulu, Hawaii 96816
Phone 732-7775
(just 3 blocks mauka of Waialae Avenue)

WHEN OPEN?   Monday-Saturday, 10:30 a.m. - 8 p.m.
Sunday, closed

GOTTA GRIND   Seared ahi with cilantro-pesto sauce,
herb-crusted mahi with lemon-crème
sauce, sautéed chicken breast with papaya
salsa and Hawaiian plates with kalua pig,
chicken long rice and lomi lomi salmon

SEATING   Keep your eyes open! (5 tables)

PARKING   No sweat! Lots of street parking

INSIDE SCOOPS   The eatery uses fresh, locally-grown
Hauula tomatoes for all of its tomato-
based items. Chicken, fish and other
meats sold by the pound. North Shore
Grinds also carries Ted's Bakery pies.
Closed on Thanksgiving, Christmas Day
and New Year's Day.

CATERING?   No

ESTABLISHED   1999

NOTES

"*I love to cook and really enjoy eating. I love to share what we offer and see our customers' happy faces.*"

Yusei Nagamine

Nuuanu Okazu-Ya

WHERE STAY?	1351 Nuuanu Avenue Honolulu, Hawaii 96817 Phone 533-6169 (between Vineyard Boulevard and Kukui Street; across from Hosoi Garden Mortuary)
WHEN OPEN?	Tuesday - Saturday, 6 a.m. - 2 p.m. Sunday, Monday & Thursday, closed
GOTTA GRIND	Okazu: Chow fun, fish cake items, kobu maki, kinpira gobo
BESIDES OKAZU	Hamburger steak, pork tofu, saimin, wonton min
SEATING	Keep your eyes open! (3 tables—but they fill up fast)
PARKING	Happy hunting! (street parking only, but an easy stroll from downtown offices)
CATERING?	No
ESTABLISHED	1978
NOTES	

"*The wafer factory started in rented space at the Kawasaki Hotel on North Kukui Street. My father was the first to use pipe gas in place of charcoal, and he manufactured hand-folded fortune cookies one-by-one.*"

Herb Ohta

Ohta Wafer Factory

Where Stay?
931 Hauoli Street
Honolulu, Hawaii 96826
Phone 949-2775

When Open?
Monday - Thursday, 8:30 a.m. - 5 p.m.
Friday, 8:30 a.m. - 4:30 p.m.
Saturday, 9 a.m. - 3 p.m.
Sunday, closed

Gotta Give
Senbei (Japanese tea cookies), fortune cookies (regular, chocolate, strawberry and green tea); ginger, mac nut, sesame seed, nori, miso; okoshi (puff rice / mac nut bars), arare (rice crackers)

Besides Omiyage
Special fortune cookies with personalized messages (regular and giant sizes)

Seating
Take-out only!

Parking
No sweat! (parking in front of the store)

Inside Scoops
Items can be packed in boxes if you're taking them on the airplane. Phone ahead to be sure we are open. No personal checks or credit cards.

Catering?
No

Established
1940

Notes

_____

_____

_____

_____

_____

_____

_____

_____

Ono Hawaiian Food

Where Stay?	726 Kapahulu Avenue Honolulu, Hawaii 96816 Phone 737-2275
When Open?	Daily, 11 a.m. - 8 p.m.
Gotta Grind	Lau lau, salt meat watercress
Seating	25 seats
Parking	Street parking along Kapahulu Avenue
Inside Scoops	Cash only
Catering?	No
Established	1962
Puka Trivia	Sueko Oh Young, the 92-year-old mother and owner, wanted to start her own business 45 years ago and not work for someone else. As a result, Ono Hawaiian Food was born. The owner today is Toyo Shimabukuro.

Notes

_____

_____

_____

_____

_____

_____

_____

_____

_____

_____

_____

_____

"*My formal cooking training was in the Army. I learned to cook with the 100th Battalion during World War II. I owned and operated several small restaurants in downtown Honolulu after the war, and also Kalakaua Drive In.*"

Jim Gusukuma

Rainbow Drive-In

WHERE STAY?   3308 Kanaina Avenue
Honolulu, Hawaii 96815
Phone 737-0177
(Look for the multi-colored building.)

WHEN OPEN?   Daily, 7:30 a.m. - 9 p.m.

GOTTA GRIND   Mixed plate, boneless chicken cutlet
with gravy, chili plate

SEATING   Make house! (7 tables)

PARKING   No sweat! (20 parking stalls, with one
handicapped stall)

INSIDE SCOOPS   Closed on Thanksgiving Week, Christmas
Day, New Year's Eve and New Year's Day.

CATERING?   No

ESTABLISHED   1961

PUKA TRIVIA   The company is headed by Harvey
Iwamura and Jim Gusukuma, sons-in-law
of founders, Seiju and Ayako Ifuku.

NOTES   _____

_____

_____

_____

_____

_____

_____

_____

_____

_____

_____

"I always feel it's important to be honest and kind to the customers, and to let them know that they are important to our daily business."

Felix Pintor

Ray's Cafe

WHERE STAY?	2033 North King Street Honolulu, Hawaii 96819 Phone 841-2771 (one block Diamond Head of Gulick Avenue; formerly Naka's)
WHEN OPEN?	Monday-Saturday, 6 a.m. - 8 p.m. Sunday, 7 a.m. - 12:30 p.m.
GOTTA GRIND	Steak and eggs, bento and the daily special
SEATING	Make house! (6 tables)
PARKING	Good luck! (street parking only.)
INSIDE SCOOPS	They also do take-out orders; sometimes closed for vacation.
CATERING?	No
ESTABLISHED	1987
NOTES	

Royal Kitchen

WHERE STAY?	100 North Beretania Street, Ste. #175 Honolulu, Hawaii 96817 Phone 524-2843 or 524-4461 (Chinese Cultural Plaza)
WHEN OPEN?	Monday - Friday, 5:30 a.m. - 5 p.m. Saturday, 6:30 a.m. - 4:30 p.m. Sunday, 6:30 a.m. - 3 p.m.
BESIDES OMIYAGE	Assortment of baked manapua, dim sum, roast duck and roast pork and Chinese dishes
SEATING	Call in advance for packing for interisland our Mainland orders. (The buns need to be cooled prior to packing).
PARKING	Half-hour free parking with validation in the back parking lot. Enter on Kukui Street.
INSIDE SCOOPS	Accepts credit cards
CATERING?	Yes
ESTABLISHED	1975
NOTES	

"*People often mistake the hash balls for andagi. But when they discover what it really is, they love it!*

Eddie Kaito

Sekiya's Restaurant & Delicatessen

WHERE STAY?	2746 Kaimuki Avenue Honolulu, Hawaii 96816 Phone 732-1656 (across Kaimuki High School)
WHEN OPEN?	Okazuya open daily, 8:30 a.m. - 4:30 p.m. Sekiya Restaurant hours: Sunday - Thursday, 8:30 a.m. - 10 p.m. Friday - Saturday, 8:30 a.m. - 11 p.m.
GOTTA GRIND	Okazu: Fried saimin, shrimp tempura, inari sushi, hash balls
BESIDES OKAZU	Oyako donburi, dine-in entrees
SEATING	Make house! Seating is available inside the restaurant.
PARKING	No sweat! (large parking lot)
INSIDE SCOOPS	Closed on Thanksgiving, Christmas and January 1st. For those who love nostalgia, Sekiya's is one of the few okazuyas that can package your okazu in a paper bento box. Credit cards accepted.
CATERING?	Yes (for small parties)
ESTABLISHED	1935 (at current location for more than 50 years)
NOTES	_____

"We both worked at the Top of Waikiki restaurant, and when the owners retired, we decided to open up our own place, offering restaurant-quality fast food. Gourmet food and local food—all homemade. We make everything from scratch.

Seiko and Jonn Aihara

Spot's Inn

WHERE STAY?	1111 Dillingham Boulevard Honolulu, Hawaii 96817 Phone 848-2770 (in Kokea Center across from Honolulu Community College)
WHEN OPEN?	Monday - Friday, 7 a.m. - 3 p.m. and 4 p.m. - 7 p.m. Saturday, 7:30 a.m. - 3 p.m. Sunday, closed
GOTTA GRIND	For breakfast: made-to-order fried rice and three-egg omelets like the "Plantation Omelet" with Portuguese sausage, green and round onion and kim chee. For lunch and dinner: Caesar salad, hamburger steak (homemade with fresh meat, not frozen patties), teri burgers and daily specials (new entrees, never before offered, added every month).
SEATING	Make house! (seating for 65)
PARKING	No sweat! (parking lot)
INSIDE SCOOPS	Closed for one or two weeks around September. Get there early because they sometimes run out of certain entrees. Accepts company checks (no personal checks); not credit cards.
CATERING?	No
ESTABLISHED	1995
PUKA TRIVIA	The restaurant is named after the Aiharas' Dalmatian, who is "lovable and loves to eat."
NOTES	

"My husband's family had an okazuya in Kalihi, but it was too small. When the owner of St. Louis Delicatessen retired, my in-laws bought the business. This was a larger okazuya and a better location—plus we looked forward to all the school kids stopping by."

Lynn Higa

St. Louis Delicatessen

WHERE STAY?	3147 Waialae Avenue Honolulu, Hawaii 96816 Phone 732-0955 (across St. Louis School, next to St. Louis Drive-In)
WHEN OPEN?	Monday, closed Tuesday-Saturday, 8 a.m. - 1:30 p.m. Sunday, closed
GOTTA GRIND	Okazu: Chow fun, fried chicken, hash, inari sushi
BESIDES OKAZU	Assortment of bento
SEATING	Keep your eyes open! (a few outdoor tables)
PARKING	No sweat! (parking lot in front of the okazuya)
INSIDE SCOOPS	They close when the food runs out, so get there early for the best selection! The okazuya also closes every now and then when the owners "need a break."
CATERING?	No
ESTABLISHED	1950s (Tsutomu and Lynn Higa took over the business in 1993.)
NOTES	_____ _____ _____ _____ _____ _____ _____ _____

"A family tradition."

Lois Ikea

The Old Saimin House
since 1963

The Old Saimin House

WHERE STAY?	1311 North King Street Honolulu, Hawaii 96817 Phone 842-7697 (next to the Kapalama Post Office)
WHEN OPEN?	Tuesday - Saturday, 11 a.m. - 2 p.m. and 6 p.m. - 11 p.m. Sunday - Monday, closed
GOTTA GRIND	Old-fashioned local saimin and BBQ sticks, wun tun min, fried saimin and fried Okinawan soba
SEATING	Make house, 8 tables
PARKING	Front of restaurant in Kapalama Shopping Plaza
CATERING?	No
ESTABLISHED	1963
NOTES	

"Our customers have been very faithful. No matter if they move to Waianae or Kalihi, whenever they're in town, they always stop by our place. They always remember us—that makes us feel good. They'll even call from Kailua and say, 'We're coming down now, so save some food for us!'"

Geraldine Matsumoto

Tsukenjo Lunch House

WHERE STAY?
705 Cooke Street
Honolulu, Hawaii 96813
Phone 597-8151
(corner of Cooke and Queen Streets)

WHEN OPEN?
Monday - Friday, 4:30 a.m. - 2:30 p.m.
Saturday - Sunday, closed

GOTTA GRIND
Roast pork, barbecue oxtail, turkey plate

SEATING
Keep your eyes open! (4 tables, 1 counter)

PARKING
Happy hunting! (street parking only)

INSIDE SCOOPS
Tsukenjo also has one lunch wagon
on the corner of Queen Street and
Ward Avenue.

CATERING?
Yes, small kine

ESTABLISHED
1959

NOTES

"In the beginning, business was tough. People didn't know what 'barbecue' was back then. We struggled the first five years. I used to give out samples and cut the burgers into fours. When we first opened, we sold hamburgers for 19 cents. We use a secret barbecue sauce for the burgers, which was developed by trial and error."

Wilfred Kanemura

W&M Bar-B-Q Burger

WHERE STAY?
3104 Waialae Avenue
Honolulu, Hawaii 96816
Phone 734-3350
(if driving Koko Head up Waialae,
it's just past City Mill)

WHEN OPEN?
Monday - Tuesday, closed
Wednesday - Friday, 10 a.m. - 4:30 p.m.
Saturday - Sunday, 9 a.m. - 4:30 p.m.

GOTTA GRIND
Barbecue hamburger, french fries

SEATING
Take-out only!

PARKING
Good luck! (When it gets crowded,
customers double park. Tip: One person
should stay in the car, while another
orders the food.)

INSIDE SCOOPS
They recommend customers call in
their orders.

CATERING?
No

ESTABLISHED
1940s (at this location since the 1980s)

NOTES
_____

_____

_____

_____

_____

_____

_____

_____

_____

_____

_____

"*Some people think we use Japanese flour, which is the reason why our breads taste different. But we use American flour. Japanese bread flour is imported from either the U.S. or Canada. Imported bread flour from Japan does not make sense at all.*"

Kosei Watanabe

Watanabe Bakery

WHERE STAY?	2065 South Beretania Street, Ste. 100 Honolulu, Hawaii 96826 Phone 946-1074
WHEN OPEN?	Monday - Saturday, 6 a.m. - 6 p.m. Sunday, closed
GOTTA GIVE	Japanese-style breads and pastries
SEATING	Two tables, but mostly take-out
PARKING	20 parking stalls shared by Mini Garden Chinese restaurant
INSIDE SCOOPS	Accepts personal checks and credit cards.
CATERING?	No
ESTABLISHED	December 2006
PUKA TRIVIA	Owner Kosei Watanabe, too young to retire after 22 years as a bakery general manager, opened this store in December 2006. "I was bored with nothing to do," he says. "I learned most of my baking and techniques from Japan."
NOTES	

"When I was in college, a friend told us about this place in Waipahu. We started selling fish, but then we noticed our Hawaiian food was selling better. Through the years, we learned to be flexible and to try make different things, like haupia brownies and cookies. A big part of our business is catering, and I really enjoy planning people's parties. When everything comes out right and everybody's happy, that's the best feeling."

Brian Yamamoto

Yama's Fish Market

WHERE STAY?   2332 Young Street
Honolulu, Hawaii 96826
Phone 941-9994
Fax 941-2600
(near the corner of Young and Isenberg
across from Stadium Mall; at former site
of Iwase Japanese bookstore)

WHEN OPEN?   Monday - Friday, 9 a.m. - 7 p.m.
Sunday, 9 a.m. - 5 p.m.

GOTTA GIVE   Hawaiian plate lunches, haupia-covered
brownies, poke

SEATING   Take-out only!

PARKING   No sweat! (small parking lot, street
parking)

INSIDE SCOOPS   Yama's delivers from Diamond Head
to the airport area for orders totaling
more than $60 (one-day advance order
required). Yama's offers Hawaiian plate
lunches and a variety of desserts and
snacks. Yama's also prepares fresh salad
and poke daily.

CATERING?   Yes

ESTABLISHED   1980 in Waipahu; 1982 in Manoa
(at current Moiliili location since 2001)

NOTES   _____

_____

_____

_____

_____

_____

_____

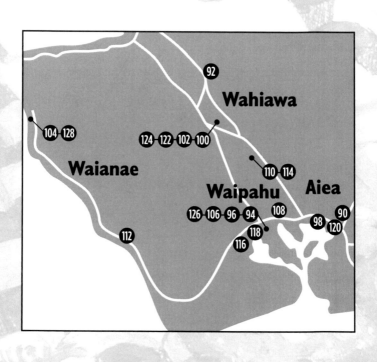

CENTRAL / LEEWARD OAHU

"I would give people my breads as gifts and then they'd ask me to bake for their fund-raisers and things. Before we knew it, it got to be more than we could handle."

Ani Tanaka

Ani's Bake Shop

WHERE STAY? 99-840 Iwaiwa Street
Aiea, Hawaii 96701
Phone: 488-2193
(Halawa Industrial Park, across from
the Halawa recreational park)

WHEN OPEN? Monday - Friday, 6 a.m. - 6 p.m.
Saturday - Sunday, 6 a.m. - 4 p.m.
(No pastries on Sunday - bread only)

GOTTA GIVE Mauna Kea (mountain-shaped cinnamon
bread), pies (sweet potato/haupia,
banana, Key lime), breads (sweet bread,
fruit-filled), banana bread, cornbread,
prune cake

SEATING Take-out only!

PARKING No sweat! (parking lot)

INSIDE SCOOPS Call in advance for orders to be taken on
the airplane; items can be packed in
Ani's "hand-carry" travel box or larger
"cargo" boxes. Accepts personal checks
and credit cards.

CATERING? No

ESTABLISHED 1983

NOTES

"We enjoy meeting visitors and local customers."

Susanna Cheung

Helemano Plantation

WHERE STAY?   64-1510 Kamehameha Highway
Wahiawa, Hawaii 96786
Phone 622-3929

WHEN OPEN?   Monday - Saturday, 11 a.m. - 2 p.m.
Sunday, 8 a.m. - 3 p.m.

GOTTA GIVE   Ginger chicken, char siu, coffee chocolate
chip cookies, macadamia nut brownies

SEATING   Make house!

PARKING   No sweat! (parking lot)

INSIDE SCOOPS   For cookies and brownies, call at least
48 hours ahead to place your order.
Accepts personal checks and credit cards.

CATERING?   Yes

ESTABLISHED   1984

NOTES

"I took over from my Dad. He started the whole thing. I love when my customers say they're so full they need to find a place to sleep."

Bobby Toguchi

Highway Inn

WHERE STAY? 94-226 Leoku Street
Waipahu, Hawaii 96797
Phone 677-4345
(in the shopping center just Ewa of
Don Quijote, Waipahu)

WHEN OPEN? Monday - Saturday, 9 a.m. - 8 p.m.
Sunday, 11 a.m. - 2 p.m.

GOTTA GRIND Butterfish 'n stew gravy, dried pipikaula,
Hawaiian beef stew, lau lau, squid lau lau

SEATING Make house! (12 tables)

PARKING No sweat! (large parking lot)

INSIDE SCOOPS Closed on Thanksgiving,
Christmas and New Year's Day and
some holidays. Accepts credit cards.

CATERING? Yes, huge selection!

ESTABLISHED 1947 (at current location since 1984)

PUKA TRIVIA Highway Inn has opened a seafood
market next door selling a variety
of fresh fish, assorted poke and
fresh vegetables. Check out the Web site
www.highwayinnonline.com. Highway Inn
is celebrating its 60th year, now in its
third generation of family owners. It
offers a taste of local flavors. It's the place
where locals go for a "taste of Hawaii."

NOTES

"People order our bentos for all different types of occasions. We've had single orders for several hundred bentos."

Lance Hirata

K's Bento-Ya

WHERE STAY?   94-164 Awalau Street
Waipahu, Hawaii 96797
Phone 671-0160
(in the two-story building on the
ewa-makai corner of Awalau and
Farrington Highway; across the street
from Jenny's Drive-In)

WHEN OPEN?   Tuesday - Saturday, 4:30 a.m. - 2 p.m.,
or when sold out.
Sunday - Monday, closed

GOTTA GRIND   Bento: fried shoyu chicken, maki sushi,
tofu patty; seven kinds of small bento and
10 kinds of large bento

SEATING   Take-out only!

PARKING   No sweat! (4 parking stalls, some
street parking)

INSIDE SCOOPS   The food often runs out as early as noon,
so get there early! K's also closes on
Thanksgiving weekend, and from
Christmas Day to New Year's Day.

CATERING?   Yes (small orders, including chicken and
maki sushi). Call for suggestions.

ESTABLISHED   1987

NOTES   _____

_____

_____

_____

_____

_____

_____

_____

"Our okazuya, I believe, was the first in this area. Without all our loyal employees, we would not have made it 'til today."

Katsumi Kazama

Kabuki Restaurant & Delicatessen

WHERE STAY?   Waimalu Shopping Center
98-020 Kamehameha Highway
Aiea, Hawaii 96701
Phone 487-2424

WHEN OPEN?   Delicatessen:
Daily, 5:30 a.m. - 1 p.m.
Tuesday, closed
Kabuki Restaurant:
Monday - Sunday,
Lunch 11 a.m. - 1:45 p.m.
Dinner 5 p.m. - 9. p.m.

GOTTA GIVE   Okazu: Inari sushi, maki sushi, kinpira gobo

BESIDES OKAZU   Sushi bar and other Japanese food

SEATING   Take-out only!

PARKING   No sweat! (Waimalu Shopping Center
parking lot)

INSIDE SCOOPS   Closes for one week every year from
January 1st. For those who love nostalgia,
Kabuki is one of the few okazuyas that
can package your okazu in the traditional
paper bento box.

CATERING?   Yes. Private party rooms are also
available.

ESTABLISHED   1965

NOTES   _____

_____

_____

_____

_____

_____

"My in-laws had the brownie recipe for a long time. It's a highly guarded secret. They don't bake them in big batches and it's made from scratch."

Dawn Takara

Kilani Bakery

WHERE STAY?   704 Kilani Avenue
Wahiawa, Hawaii 96786
Phone 621-5662

WHEN OPEN?   Daily, 4:30 a.m. - 6:30 p.m.

GOTTA GIVE   Brownies, sweetbread, prune loaf, bread
pudding, an pan, sweet potato turnover,
custard pie

BESIDES OMIYAGE   Full-service bakery sells a large
assortment of pastries, plus decorated
cakes for birthdays, weddings and other
special occasions.

SEATING   Take-out only!

PARKING   No sweat! (small parking lot)

INSIDE SCOOPS   Call in advance for large orders or if
traveling to a Neighbor Island. Items can
be packed for travel. Accepts credit cards.

CATERING?   No

ESTABLISHED   1959

NOTES   _____

_____

_____

_____

_____

_____

_____

_____

_____

_____

_____

> "This is the most enjoyable business for me. I've met so many wonderful people. I wish I had started this business 20 years earlier. I'm getting along in age."

Gladys Okamura

Kitchen Delight

WHERE STAY?
553 California Avenue
Wahiawa, Hawaii 96786
Phone 622-3463
(corner of California and
Walker Avenues)

WHEN OPEN?
Monday - Friday, 5 a.m. - 2 p.m.
Saturday - Sunday & holidays, 6 a.m. - 2 p.m.

GOTTA GRIND
Okazu: Mochiko chicken and teri chicken
(both boneless, skinless), fried saimin,
fish patty, chicken skin chips

BESIDES OKAZU
Breakfast, saimin, plate lunch,
Hawaiian food

SEATING
Make house! (5 tables)

PARKING
Happy Hunting! (street parking only)

CATERING?
Yes

ESTABLISHED
1995

OKAZUYA TRIVIA
Long-time Wahiawa residents may
remember Kitchen Delight at its former
location on the corner of Cane Street
and California Avenue from 1973 to 1986.
After a fire destroyed most of the
building her okazuya occupied, owner
Gladys Okamura decided to close her
business and focus her energy on
catering. The okazuya itch returned in
1995 when an old neighborhood saimin
shop closed down—it was the perfect
location for her new okazuya.

NOTES

"Lahilahi Drive-In and Killer Shrimp are owned by the Saballa family from Makaha. We believe in helping the children in our community with educational and community sports functions."

Fabian Saballa

Lahilahi Drive-In

WHERE STAY?   84-1150 Farrington Highway
Waianae, Hawaii 96792
Phone 696-4811
(one block past the 7-Eleven on the right)

WHEN OPEN?   Drive-In:
Monday - Friday, 7 a.m. - 8 p.m.
Saturday, 7 a.m. - 3 p.m.
Sunday, 8 a.m. - 3 p.m.

Poke Shop:
Monday, closed
Tuesday - Sunday, 10 a.m. - 7 p.m.

Okazuya:
Weekends only

GOTTA GRIND   Killer shrimp scampi, fish burgers,
hamburger steak, saimin, Korean chicken,
chicken katsu and kalbi short ribs.

SEATING   Make house! (4 tables with 5 chairs)

PARKING   No sweat! Parking lot in front.

INSIDE SCOOPS   At Lahilahi Drive-In, formally Makaha
Drive-In, you'll find its popular Killer
Shrimp Truck, poke shop and weekend
okazuya. The drive-in makes its own
sauces and BBQ-ers are welcome to stop
by and pick up marinated picnic meats for
easy grilling.

CATERING?   Yes

ESTABLISHED   2004

NOTES

"I love making good food that people enjoy."

Rene Paulo, Jr.

HAWAIIAN MENU
$7.95 PER HEAD

KALUA PIG
TERIYAKI CHICKEN
CHICKEN LONG RICE
SQUID LUAU
LOMI SALMON
RICE
POI
HAUPIA
PINEAPPLE
SWEET POTATO
JUICE

W/POKE
(ADDL. 11.05 PER HEAD)

*PAPER GOODS INCLUDED
(WITH A MINIMUM ORDER FOR 50 PEOPLE)

CATERING

Laverne's Catering and Take-Out

WHERE STAY?	94-752C Hikimoe Street Waipahu, Hawaii 96797 Phone 678-1678 or 386-8965 (cell) (behind Times Super Market)
WHEN OPEN?	Monday - Saturday, 10:30 a.m. - 7 p.m. Sunday, closed
GOTTA GRIND	Number 1 Combo (kalua pig, chicken long rice, squid luau, rice, lomi salmon, haupia); Number 5 Combo (kalua pig and lau lau); squid luau; shoyu chicken
SEATING	Take-out and dine in
PARKING	Happy hunting! (lots of parking)
INSIDE SCOOPS	Closed on Thanksgiving, Christmas Day and New Year's Day.
CATERING?	Yes
ESTABLISHED	2000
PUKA TRIVIA	Laverne owns the restaurant with her husband, Rene Paulo, Jr., of the musical Paulo family.
NOTES	

"I used to own a restaurant and learned about the hotel industry from school. What's kept me in business is hard work. But I enjoy serving popular local food and making friends."

Goro Tokiwa

Leeward Grill

WHERE STAY?	850 Kamehameha Highway, #210 Pearl City, Hawaii 96782 Phone 456-4488 (in Leeward Bowl located in Pearl City Shopping Center)
WHEN OPEN?	Daily, 8 a.m. - Midnight
GOTTA GRIND	Hamburger steak, beef of pork adobo, chopped steak and kalua pork with lomi lomi salmon
SEATING	Make house! 3 tables in the snack shop area, and 3 long tables in the bowling alley
PARKING	No sweat! (lots of parking in the Pearl City Shopping Center)
INSIDE SCOOPS	Closed annually, from Dec. 31 - Jan. 4.
CATERING?	Available for parties in the bowling center and the bar. Most popular service is the Children's Birthday Package. Includes bowling and food.
ESTABLISHED	2005
NOTES	

"Lum's Inn is known for its friendly and personal service. A lot of the same customers have been coming in for years. We really enjoy serving our friends and family, and we hope to continue for many years. We think we have that special touch that makes all who visit us want to come back."

Jeffrey Souza

Lum's Inn

WHERE STAY?	95-390 Kuahelani Avenue Mililani, Hawaii 96789 Phone 623-9700 (Mililani Shopping Center, near First Hawaiian Bank)
WHEN OPEN?	Monday, 8 a.m. - 4 p.m. Tuesday-Friday, 8 a.m. - 7 p.m. Saturday, 8 a.m. - 2 p.m. Sunday, closed
GOTTA GRIND	Teri beef and chicken mixed plate, teri beef and shrimp combo, teri chicken and shrimp combo
SEATING	Take-out only!
PARKING	No sweat! (big parking lot)
INSIDE SCOOPS	The secret-recipe teri sauce marinade is also for sale.
CATERING?	No
ESTABLISHED	1979
PUKA TRIVIA	Lum's was formerly known as Inn & Out.
NOTES	

"Our goal is to give back to the community. We wouldn't be here if it wasn't for their support. We tried to offer better prices and one-stop shopping."

Marilyn Dumancas

Mike's Bake Shop

WHERE STAY?	87-1650 Farrington Highway Waianae, Hawaii 96792 Phone 668-7133
WHEN OPEN?	Monday, closed Tuesday, 5:30 a.m. - 12:30 p.m. Wednesday, closed Thursday - Friday, 5:30 a.m. - 1:30 p.m. Saturday - Sunday, 6 a.m. - 1 p.m.
GOTTA GIVE	Rainbow cake, butter rolls, glazed doughnuts
BESIDES OMIYAGE	Frozen meats (chicken, beef, pork), poke, shrimp, dried fish
SEATING	Take-out only!
PARKING	No sweat!
INSIDE SCOOPS	Cakes need to be ordered 3 days in advance and must be kept refrigerated. Accepts personal checks and credit cards.
CATERING?	Yes
ESTABLISHED	1985
NOTES	

WELCOME TO THE MILILANI GOLF CLUB RESTAURANT

ALONZO'S HAWAIIAN BEEF STEAK

OXTAIL SOUP	CHINESE STYLE AHI BELLY
RIBEYE STEAK	KIMCHEE FRIED RICE
LOCO MOCO	KALBI
CHICKEN WINGS	MAHIMAHI
GRILLED SALMON	HAMBURGER STEAK
STEAMED MULLET	
TERI BEEF OR CHICKEN	
CHICKEN OR BEEF CHOPSTEAK	
KALUA PORK & CABBAGE	
BREADED OR GRILLED PORK CHOPS	
1 LB. SIZZLING HAMBURGER STEAK	

' PUPU PLATTER '
HAWAIIAN STYLE 'PHILLY STEAK' SANDWICH

FOOD MADE TO ORDER

HOURS 6:00 - 8:00PM
KITCHEN CLOSES AT 7:30
FOOD MADE TO ORDER

"FILLY" PINO FOODS

SERVED 11:30 - 7:00

- - - 25 30 MIN. COOKING TIME - - -

PANCIT	CHICKEN PAPAYA
SARI SARI	PINAKBET

FOOD MADE TO ORDER

CRISPY PATA	DINUGUAN
CRISPY TRIPE	ADOBO :
	PORK OR CHICKEN

"We pride ourselves in providing good service with the very best of 'local style' food that takes place in a casual, friendly and family-oriented environment."

Mel Abrazado

Mililani Golf Club Restaurant

WHERE STAY?
95-176 Kuahelani Avenue
Mililani, Hawaii 96789
Phone 625-2256

WHEN OPEN?
Daily, 6 a.m. - 8 p.m.
Last call at 7:30 p.m.

GOTTA GRIND
Alonzo's Hawaiian beef steak. The meat practically melts in your mouth. It has a full BBQ flavor that keeps customers coming back for more.

SEATING
As a restaurant that caters to golfers, seating is arranged for foursomes, but tables can be joined together for 10 or more. The back area is available for 50 people for semi-private parties.

PARKING
Ample parking shared with the golf course.

INSIDE SCOOPS
Accepts credit cards

CATERING?
Yes. The restaurant began as a catering business.

ESTABLISHED
2002

PUKA TRIVIA
Brothers Mel and Francis "Alonzo" Abrazado launched a catering business in 1995, serving the west side of the island. Mel had 35 years of experience as a United Airlines flight attendant. Francis "Alonzo" enjoyed cooking for his family and was never shy at experimenting with flavors. As customer demand grew, the brothers opened Mililani Golf Club Restaurant. Alonzo, who created the majority of menu items, focuses on the food's freshness and flavor. The Abrazado brothers are happy to hear customers say that the food takes them back to good, home-cooked meals.

"First, my mom and dad taught me how to cook, and then came the Big 3: Chefs Emeril Lagasse, Alan Wong and Sam Choy. I started my own business to be closer to home, spend more time with family and control my own destiny. The secret to success is to be humble and never forget where you came from."

Elmer Guzman

Poke Stop

WHERE STAY?	94-050 Farrington Highway, E-4 Waipahu, Hawaii 96797 Phone 676-8100
WHEN OPEN?	Monday - Saturday, 8 a.m. - 7 p.m. Sunday, 8 a.m. - 5 p.m,
GOTTA GRIND	Fresh Island fish, gourmet plate lunch and fresh poke
SEATING	Covered outdoor tables
PARKING	No sweat! Parking at the Waipahu Town Center
INSIDE SCOOPS	Accepts credit cards and EBT cards
CATERING?	Yes
ESTABLISHED	July 2005
NOTES	

"I like our customers. We get to talk story. And we have customers who come in every day. Some of them come for breakfast and lunch. It's so great to just talk to them."

Agnes Ishii

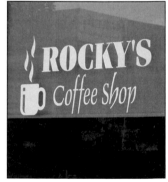

Rocky's Coffee Shop

WHERE STAY?
94-316 Waipahu Depot Road
Waipahu, Hawaii 96797
Phone 677-3842
(across the street from the old
Arakawa's store)

WHEN OPEN?
Monday - Wednesday and Friday,
4:30 a.m. - 2 p.m.
Sunday, 5 a.m. - 12:30 p.m.
Thursday, closed

GOTTA GRIND
Fried rice omelette, hot cakes, hamburger
steak, cornbread

SEATING
Make house! (12 stools and several
comfortable booths)

PARKING
No sweat! (a small parking lot in the back,
plus street parking)

INSIDE SCOOPS
A couple of years ago, Rocky's moved
one door down on the street and now
resides in an updated space. Breakfast
served all day long; closed on Thanksgiving,
Christmas Day and New Year's, as well as
one week's annual vacation (varies).

CATERING?
No

ESTABLISHED
1960

NOTES
_____

_____

_____

_____

_____

_____

_____

_____

"Although I had 15 years of restaurant business experience under my belt, I had never cooked until we opened Sakura. Now I cook almost everything!"

Lloyd Sakuda

Sakura Japanese Delicatessen & Catering

WHERE STAY?	Aiea Town Square 99-080 Kauhale Street, Suite C1 Aiea, Hawaii 96701 Phone 484-1141 (in the shopping center next to Aiea Public Library)
WHEN OPEN?	Monday, closed Tuesday - Saturday, 6:30 a.m. - 2 p.m. Sunday, 6:30 a.m. - 1:30 p.m.
GOTTA GRIND	Corn beef hash, baked mahi, mochiko chicken, seafood casserole and misoyaki butterfish
BESIDES OKAZU	Tofu salad, Oriental chicken salad, assorted bento, plate lunch
SEATING	Make house! (3 tables with 4 chairs each)
PARKING	No sweat! (lots of parking in the shopping center)
INSIDE SCOOPS	Closes for vacation the first week of January. They accept local personal checks, and they continue to replenish the food throughout the day.
CATERING?	Yes
ESTABLISHED	1993
NOTES	

"My grandparents had a saimin stand in Haleiwa while I was growing up. I always dreamed of having one of my own. I learned a lot from my uncle, whose specialty was making noodles."

Ross Shigeoka

Shige's Saimin Stand

Where Stay?	70 Kukui Street Wahiawa, Hawaii 96786 Phone 621-3621 (in the strip mall on Kamehameha Highway across from Zippy's)
When Open?	Monday - Thursday, 10 a.m. - 10 p.m. Friday - Saturday, 10 a.m. - Midnight Sunday, closed
Gotta Grind	Won ton mein, hamburger steak plate, vegetable saimin, barbecue stick
Seating	Make house! (seats 45 people)
Parking	No sweat! (parking lot and street parking)
Inside Scoops	Take-out orders are packed nicely, with noodles in a separate container from the soup base so they won't get overcooked.
Catering?	No
Established	1990
Notes	

"We offer good, home-cooked meals—just like Mother used to make. In fact, we use all my mother's and my aunt's recipes. They originally owned the Kemoo Coffee Shop at the old bus station in Wahiawa—where Long's is now. They were there for 30 years before Sunnyside. They were a hole-in-the-wall in the bus station, too, but they were really busy!"

Lucy Shimonishi

Sunnyside

WHERE STAY? 1017 Kilani Avenue
Wahiawa, Hawaii 96786
Phone 621-7188
(corner of Kilani and Cane Streets,
next to the park)

WHEN OPEN? Monday - Saturday, 6 a.m. - 6 p.m.
Saturday, 6 a.m. - 4 p.m.
Sunday, closed

GOTTA GRIND Homemade hamburgers, Korean plate
lunches, fried rice special for breakfast

GOTTA GIVE Fruit and cream pies. Don't miss the
chocolate cream pie!

SEATING Make house! (10 tables)

PARKING No sweat! (small parking lot)

INSIDE SCOOPS Biggest sellers are the homemade pies—
especially the chocolate cream. Pies sell
out quickly over the holidays, so place
your order early! Thanksgiving pies can be
ordered as early as November 1;
Christmas and New Year's orders are
taken beginning December 1. Sunnyside
is closed on Thanksgiving, Christmas and
New Year's.

CATERING? No

ESTABLISHED 1977

NOTES _____

_____

_____

_____

_____

_____

"Quality foods with a friendly smile has been our motto for the past 24 years."

Mel Tanioka

Tanioka's Seafoods & Catering

WHERE STAY?   94-903 Farrington Highway
Waipahu, Hawaii 96797
Phone 671-3779

WHEN OPEN?   Monday - Saturday, 9 a.m. - 5 p.m.
Sunday, 9 a.m. - 3 p.m.

GOTTA GRIND   Okazu: Inari sushi, poke, andagi

SEATING   Take-out only!

PARKING   No sweat! (parking lot)

BESIDES OMIYAGE   They sell okazu items and offer an
extensive seafood menu

CATERING?   Yes

ESTABLISHED   1978

INSIDE SCOOPS   *Honolulu Advertiser* 2006 Award–Best of
the Best Poke & Seafood. *Honolulu
Magazine* 2007 Award–Best Poke.
Accepts personal checks and credit cards.

NOTES   _____

_____

_____

_____

_____

_____

_____

_____

_____

_____

_____

Waianae Drive In

WHERE STAY?
89-859 Farrington Highway
Waianae, Hawaii 96792
Phone 696-6070
(Corner of Farrington Highway and Old
Plantation Road; light blue building with
yellow tile)

WHEN OPEN?
Daily, 10 a.m. - 6 p.m.

GOTTA GRIND
Cheeseburgers, french fries (with special
sauce by request only); they peel their
own potatoes every day

SEATING
Take-out only!

PARKING
Happy hunting! (small parking lot)

INSIDE SCOOPS
Closed on Thanksgiving, Christmas Day
and New Year's Day.

CATERING?
No

ESTABLISHED
Late 1950s

NOTES

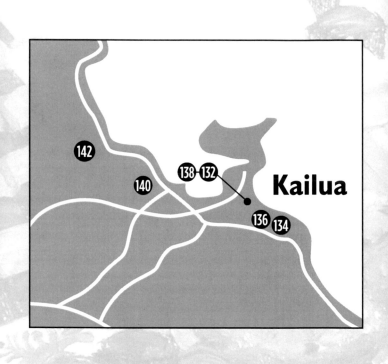

Windward Oahu

"Since taking over
the shop 15 years ago,
we've grown and have
developed a loyal clientele.
Through imagination and
creativity, we've developed
more products. One of the
most enjoyable aspects?
I get to eat a lot! Actually,
I think most people do
this because they really
believe in the product they
put out there."

Non DeMello
(co-owner with
Christian Sorli)

Agnes' Portuguese Bake Shop

WHERE STAY?	46 Hoolai Street Kailua, Hawaii 96734 Phone 262-5367
WHEN OPEN?	Tuesday - Saturday, 6 a.m. - 6 p.m. Sunday, 6 a.m. - 2 p.m. Monday, closed
GOTTA GIVE	Malassadas, sweetbread, Portuguese and European artisan breads, Molokai Mud Pie (macadamia nut/chocolate chip pie)
SEATING	Make house! (7 tables, including 3 Internet computer stations)
PARKING	No sweat! (parking lot)
INSIDE SCOOPS	Malassadas made "fresh to order," so call in advance for large orders. Accepts personal checks and credit cards.
CATERING?	Yes, (platters of pastries for breakfast meetings, etc.)
ESTABLISHED	1972
NOTES	

"It's rough work and it can get very tiring, especially with the long and early hours, but we enjoy what we're doing."

Howard Ishikawa

Blossom's Okazuya

WHERE STAY?
1090 Keolu Drive, Suite 109
Kailua, Hawaii 96734
Phone 263-3338
Fax 263-5528
(in the same shopping center as Keolu
Center Cinemas - Wallace Theatres in
Enchanted Lake)

WHEN OPEN?
Tuesday - Saturday, 6 a.m. - 2 p.m.
Monday and Sunday, closed

GOTTA GRIND
Okazu: Sesame chicken, maki sushi,
ginger-shoyu pork

BESIDES OKAZU
Bento, plate lunch, poke, fresh fish

SEATING
Take-out only!

PARKING
No sweat! (shopping center parking lot)

INSIDE SCOOPS
New owners, Laverne Jowers and Chad
Hashimoto, close shop when the food
runs out, as early as 1 p.m. so get there
early for the best selection!

CATERING?
Yes (for small parties)

ESTABLISHED
1990 (at current location since 1997)

NOTES
_____

_____

_____

_____

_____

_____

_____

_____

_____

_____

"Home of the original macadamia nut pancake sauce"

"We don't know where all the people come from, but they appear. My brother and I thank the Lord for blessing us with this great dream that we made reality."

Rick Kiakona

Boots & Kimo's Homestyle Kitchen

WHERE STAY?   131 Hekili Street, Ste. 102
Kailua, Hawaii 96734
Phone 263-7929

WHEN OPEN?   Tuesday - Friday, 7 a.m. - 2 p.m.
Saturday - Sunday, 6:30 a.m. - 2:30 p.m.
Open on main holidays that fall
on Mondays.

GOTTA GRIND   Macadamia nut pancakes

SEATING   34 seats

PARKING   Park across the street at the bowling
alley or on the street

INSIDE SCOOPS   Cash only

CATERING?   Yes. For small parties only. Ask for details.

ESTABLISHED   June 18, 1994. Father's Day!

PUKA TRIVIA   Brothers Rick and Jesse Kiakona opened
their restaurant more than 12 years ago
and named it after their Dad "Boots"
and their Uncle Kimo from Maui. Boots
was the head chef at the old Coco's
restaurant. Uncle Kimo owned his own
gazebo in Napili Shores from 1980 to
1988. Customers keep coming back
for the mac pancakes, omelettes and
pulehu ribs.

NOTES   _____

_____

_____

_____

_____

_____

"*My husband and I are originally from Japan. And you won't find 'okazuyas' in Japan. The okazuya is local— the food is different from Japanese food. My customers taught me how to cook this way—if I make and they don't like it, I try again until they like it.*"

Miyoko Kochi

Kuulei Delicatessen

WHERE STAY?
418 Kuulei Road
Kailua, Hawaii 96734
Phone 261-5321
Fax 261-5321 (call before faxing)
(next to the Shell gas station at the entrance of Kailua town on the corner of Oneawa Street and Kuulei Road)

WHEN OPEN?
Tuesday - Friday, 6:30 a.m. - 1 p.m.
Saturday, 8 a.m. - 1 p.m.
Sunday - Monday, closed

GOTTA GRIND
Okazu: Fried saimin, chowfun, shoyu butterfish, garlic chicken, tempura poke, furikake salmon, nishime, andagi, pasteles, lau lau, beef stew and a whole lot more!

SEATING
Make house! (6 tables)

PARKING
Street parking and public parking (entrance between McDonald's and Lucy Grill)

INSIDE SCOOPS
Closes for one week after New Year's. Accepts credit cards and debit cards.

CATERING?
Yes

ESTABLISHED
1972, under new management since 2004

NOTES
_____

_____

_____

_____

_____

_____

_____

_____

"The logo's kanji character means 'happiness' and the circle around it signifies 'complete.' We hope our customers are completely happy when they enjoy our okazu."

Eloise Holt

Maruki-Tei

WHERE STAY? Windward Mall
46-056 Kamehameha Highway
Kaneohe, Hawaii 96744
Phone 235-4445

WHEN OPEN? Monday - Saturday, 10 a.m. - 9 p.m.
(okazu section closes at 8 p.m.)
Sunday, 10 a.m. - 5 p.m.

GOTTA GRIND Okazu: Sesame chicken, sushi, tempura,
mac/potato salad

BESIDES OKAZU Plate lunch (beef stew, saimin, sweet sour
spare ribs, chicken tofu with long rice,
etc.), Hawaiian food

SEATING Make house! (6 tables and seats on the
counter—and, of course, places to sit
in the mall)

PARKING No sweat! (Windward Mall parking lot)

INSIDE SCOOPS They continue to replenish the food
throughout the day and the saimin soup is
made with their "old-fashioned" recipe.

CATERING? Yes

ESTABLISHED 1982

OKAZUYA TRIVIA In 2007, Maruki-Tei enjoyed it's 25th year
at the Windward Mall. However, the
company has a total of 47 wonderful
years in Kaneohe.

NOTES

_____

_____

_____

_____

_____

"I grew up working in the business, and it's become a way of life I truly enjoy."

Cynthia Tobaru

Masa & Joyce

WHERE STAY?	45-582 Kamehameha Highway Kaneohe, Hawaii 96744 Phone 235-6129 (by Koolau Farmers and Kin Wah Chinese restaurant)
WHEN OPEN?	Wednesday - Friday, 9 a.m. - 6 p.m. Saturday, 9 a.m. - 4 p.m. Sunday, 9 a.m. - 2 p.m. Monday - Tuesday, closed
GOTTA GRIND	Okazu: Ahi patty, California roll, sweet potato mochi, hot dog/Spam musubi, fried noodles and chcken katsu
BESIDES OKAZU	Hawaiian plate lunch, sashimi, poke, andagi
SEATING	Make house! (6 tables)
PARKING	No sweat! (large parking lot)
INSIDE SCOOPS	Closed the first week in January. Accepts credit cards.
CATERING?	Yes
ESTABLISHED	1984
NOTES	

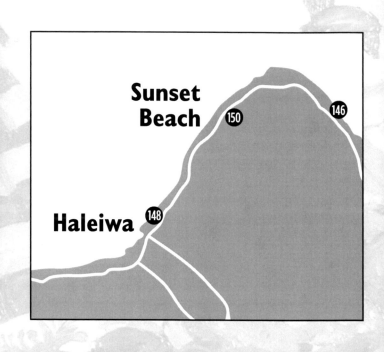

NORTH SHORE

"My mother, Amy, taught me how to cook. She always said to 'make sure everything is tasty' and to make sure it looks good, too!"

Diane Huddy

Amy's By the Greene

WHERE STAY?   56-485 Kamehameha Highway
Kahuku, Hawaii 96731
Phone 293-8896
(across Kahuku High School)

WHEN OPEN?   Monday - Friday, 7 a.m. - 3 p.m.
Saturday, 8:30 a.m. - 1 p.m.
Sunday, closed
(Open on school holidays from
8:30 a.m. - 3 p.m.)

GOTTA GRIND   Mushroom burger, shrimp burger, ham
burger steak and onions, deep-fried teri
chicken, ulu fries (when in season) with
ranch dressing, Tahitian luau leaf lau lau
(when in season) with pork, beef and
turkey tail

SEATING   Make house! (4 picnic tables)

PARKING   Happy hunting! (small parking lot)

CATERING?   No

ESTABLISHED   1998

NOTES

_____

_____

_____

_____

_____

_____

_____

_____

_____

_____

148

"*My family is originally from the North Shore. We wanted to own our own business and realized Haleiwa didn't have an okazuya. The hours are long and it's hard work, but we're enjoying every minute of it and we love the community.*"

Deann Sakuoka

North Shore Country Okazu & Bento

WHERE STAY?	Haleiwa Shopping Center 66-197C Kamehameha Highway Haleiwa, Hawaii 96712 Phone 637-0055
WHEN OPEN?	Daily, 5 a.m. - 1 p.m.
GOTTA GRIND	Okazu: Fishcake, fried chicken, shoyu chicken
BESIDES OKAZU	Freshly made salads, smoothies and daily specials
SEATING	Make house! (4 tables, but okazu tastes even better at the beach, which is only a few minutes away!)
PARKING	No sweat! (lots of parking at Haleiwa Shopping Center)
CATERING?	Yes
ESTABLISHED	1999
OKAZUYA TRIVIA	North Shore Country Okazu is a family affair owned by two sisters—Janelle and Deann Sakuoka.
NOTES	

"My parents opened the Sunset Beach store in 1956. After high school, I attended Leeward Community College's Food Service Program. I have always enjoyed experimenting and trying to create a new and different product. The creation of the chocolate haupia pie came about by accident. One day there was some haupia cream left over from a cake order and some leftover chocolate cream from the chocolate pies. I decided to layer each of them in a pie shell—and it took off from there!"

Ted Nakamura

Ted's Bakery

Where Stay?	59-024 Kamehameha Highway Haleiwa, Hawaii 96712 Phone 638-8207 (Sunset Beach)
When Open?	Bakery: Monday - Sunday, 7 a.m. - 6 p.m. Restaurant: Monday - Thursday, 7 a.m. - 4 p.m. Friday - Sunday, 7 a.m. - 5 p.m.
Gotta Give	Assortment of pies (chocolate, haupia, chocolate cream, strawberry cream), bakery items (eclairs, big butter rolls, big cinnamon rolls, carrot cake)
Besides Omiyage	Ono plate lunches, hot and cold sandwiches and breakfast
Seating	7 tables with umbrellas, seats up to 28
Parking	No sweat! (14 stalls)
Inside Scoops	Ted's now offers a selection of 9-inch cakes. Available every day. For interisland travel, they suggest you bring a bag that can fit in the overhead compartment; fill it with blue ice to keep the pies chilled. Call in advance for big orders. Accepts personal checks and credit cards.
Catering?	No
Established	1956 (bakery opened in 1987)
Notes	_____ _____ _____ _____ _____ _____

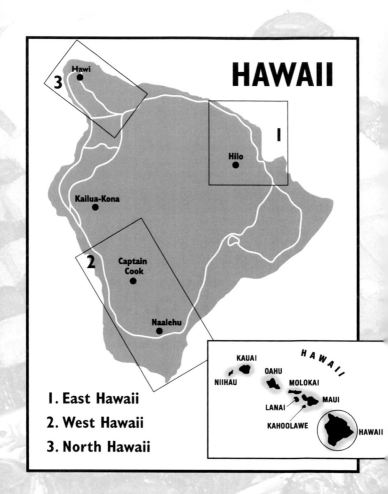

HAWAII

3 Hawi

1

Hilo

Kailua-Kona

2 Captain Cook

Naalehu

1. East Hawaii
2. West Hawaii
3. North Hawaii

KAUAI

NIIHAU

OAHU

MOLOKAI

LANAI

MAUI

KAHOOLAWE

H A W A I I

HAWAII

THE BIG ISLAND

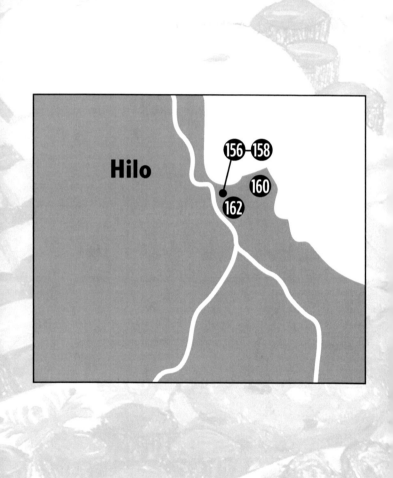

East Hawaii

"There was a time when I was ready to jump off a bridge! At that time, if you told me that I would accomplish what we've done so far, I'd have said you were nuts!"

Allan Ikawa

Big Island Candies

WHERE STAY?	585 Hinano Street Hilo, Hawaii 96720 Phone 961-2199
WHEN OPEN?	Daily, 8:30 a.m. - 5 p.m.
GOTTA GIVE	Chocolate-dipped shortbread cookies, macadamia nut chocolates, brownies, biscotti and much more!
BESIDES OMIYAGE	Island-made ice cream, beverages
SEATING	Keep your eyes open! (3 benches)
PARKING	No sweat! (parking lot)
INSIDE SCOOPS	Orders can be placed on-line at www.bigislandcandies.com or by calling toll-free 1-800-935-5510. Accepts personal checks and credit cards.
CATERING?	No
ESTABLISHED	1977
NOTES	

"We have operated our business for about 20 years. About five years ago, a friend confided that some thought we wouldn't make it, that we'd fold soon after we started. We were stunned to hear this because, though we went through some really rough times, the thought of failing never entered our minds. The moral of the story is that birds can fly because they think they can!"

Judy Jakahi

George's Meat Market

WHERE STAY?
28 Hoku Street
Hilo, Hawaii 96720
Phone 935-8225

WHEN OPEN?
Monday, Tuesday, Thursday, Friday,
9:30 a.m. - 5 p.m.
Wednesday, 9 a.m. - 12:45 p.m.
Saturday, 8:30 a.m. - 2 p.m.
Sunday, closed

GOTTA GIVE
Vacuum-packed "heat n' serve" or "ready-
to-cook" items: kal bi steak, kal bi oxtail,
smoked pork ribs, teri chicken, miso ahi,
slavanic steak, oven-ready prime rib, abalone

BESIDES OMIYAGE
George's sells an assortment of U.S.D.A.
Choice and Prime graded beef, pork,
seafood and chicken for everyday
cooking. Many items are prepared to
make it easier for the chef in the family,
such as garlic butter that comes with the
jumbo scallops, marinated items that can
be used for stir-frying, or seasoned
flour/cornstarch blend for the
soft-shell crab.

SEATING
Take-out only!

PARKING
No sweat! (parking lot)

INSIDE SCOOPS
Customers should indicate whether the
products are going off-island, so that they
can help in packaging the items for travel.
George's also closes for a week-and-a-half
each in the spring, summer and fall.
Accepts personal checks and credit cards.

CATERING?
No, but they will cook/smoke items, such
as their Oven Ready Prime Rib upon
request (if the quantity is large enough).

ESTABLISHED
1949 by George Jakahi, owned and run by
Stacey and Brian Mukai

"*This business was a success before we bought it; we're just hoping to continue it. Lots of people take our fish-cake, nori chicken and sushi home as omiyage to Honolulu and the Mainland. If you open it on the plane, everyone says, 'Oooo, smells like Hilo Lunch Shop!'*"

Junette Nakamura

Hilo Lunch Shop

WHERE STAY?   421 Kalanikoa St.
Hilo, Hawaii 96720
Phone 935-8273

WHEN OPEN?   Tuesday - Saturday, 5:30 a.m. - 1 p.m.
Sunday, closed

GOTTA GRIND   Okazu: Cone sushi, nori chicken, nishime
and fishcake

SEATING   Take-out only!

PARKING   No sweat! About 10 parking stalls in lot.

INSIDE SCOOPS   Closed the first week of the year.
Accepts personal checks and credit cards.

CATERING?   Yes

ESTABLISHED   1984

NOTES

"*I've always wanted a job that I would never get bored with. Look what happened—I'm never bored! The secret to the success of Nori's is a lot of hard work, experimenting—and a pinch of craziness!*"

Beth-An Nishijima

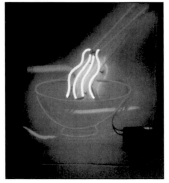

Nori's Saimin & Snacks

WHERE STAY?	688 Kinoole Street, Ste. 124 Hilo, Hawaii 96720 Phone 935-9133
WHEN OPEN?	Tuesday - Saturday, 10:30 a.m. - Midnight Sunday, 10:30 a.m. - 9:30 p.m. Monday, closed
GOTTA GIVE	Chocolate mochi cake, teri tako, chocolate mochi cookies, strawpia pie, mustard cabbage koko, Chex mix
BESIDES OMIYAGE	Local food, lots of noodle dishes, saimin (including "sizzling" saimin), tofu steak, salmon steak
SEATING	Make house! (more than 60 chairs)
PARKING	No sweat! (parking lot)
INSIDE SCOOPS	Advance ordering is recommended for big orders. Accepts credit cards, but no personal checks.
CATERING?	Yes
ESTABLISHED	1983
NOTES	

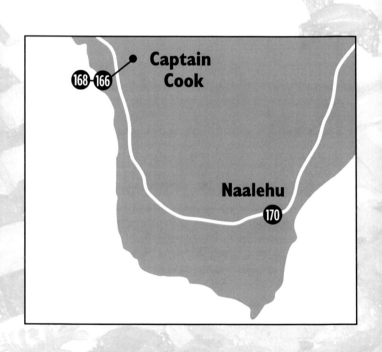

WEST HAWAII

"When Mr. and Mrs. Deguchi, Cindee's parents, retired after 50 years in the potato chip business, we bought the business from them. Mr. Deguchi taught me about the potato chip business and how to master the technique of cooking kettle-style potato chips. One good lesson I learned is that when the oil splashes on you, it is very hot!"

**Jerome Furukawa
(owner with wife Cindee)**

Kona Chips

WHERE STAY?	82-6155 Mamalahoa Highway Captain Cook, Hawaii 96704 Phone 323-3785
WHEN OPEN?	Monday - Tuesday, 8:30 a.m. - 5 p.m. Wednesday, 8:30 a.m. - 3 p.m. Thursday - Friday, 8:30 a.m. - 5 p.m. Saturday, 9 a.m. - 2 p.m. Sunday, closed
GOTTA GIVE	Kona chips, furikake chips (one-of-a-kind in the nation!)
BESIDES OMIYAGE	Cookies, cracked seed, mochi crunch; also manju during the Christmas holiday season. A sister company, Petroglyphs in Paradise, features a line of snacks and gift baskets.
SEATING	Take-out only!
PARKING	No sweat! (street parking, parking lot)
INSIDE SCOOPS	If you call in your order early, they will have it boxed and ready to go. They close one week a year to take their employees to Las Vegas. Accepts personal checks and credit cards.
CATERING?	No
ESTABLISHED	1991
NOTES	

Manago Hotel Restaurant

WHERE STAY?
82-6155 Mamalahoa Highway
Captain Cook, Hawaii 96704
Phone 323-2642

WHEN OPEN?
Daily, 7 a.m. - 9 p.m.
Lunch: 11 a.m. - 2 p.m.
Dinner: 5 p.m. - 7:30 p.m.
Closed for one week after Mother's Day.

GOTTA GRIND
Pork chops and fried opelu

SEATING
Ample seating

PARKING
Two parking lots

INSIDE SCOOPS
Accepts credit cards; no personal checks

CATERING?
No

ESTABLISHED
1917

PUKA TRIVIA
Dwight and Cheryl Manago are the owners. Their grandparents started the business in 1917.

NOTES
_____

_____

_____

_____

_____

_____

_____

_____

_____

_____

_____

_____

"My mother taught me a lot about food preparation and baking. She owned her own bakery and restaurant. The secret to my success is having knowledge of the total operation from accounting and baking bread to dealing with customers in retail. I also attribute our success to my wonderful staff."

Connie Koi

Punaluu Bakeshop

WHERE STAY?	95-5642 Mamalahoa Highway Naalehu, Hawaii 96772 Phone 929-7343
WHEN OPEN?	Daily, 9 a.m. - 5 p.m.
GOTTA GIVE	Sweetbreads, including traditional, guava and taro. Also, try Kalakoa (a combination loaf of mango, taro and guava), an pan (bean-filled) and coconut pan.
BESIDES OMIYAGE	Punaluu macadamia nut shortbread cookies, original macadamia nut or infused with an array of tropical flavors, such as coconut, lilikoi glazed, crème or fruit filled and, of course, traditional sugared
SEATING	Open-air gazebos, seating for 80
PARKING	No sweat! (parking lot with 25 stalls)
INSIDE SCOOPS	Call in advance for large orders. Accepts personal checks and credit cards.
CATERING?	No
ESTABLISHED	1991
NOTES	

171

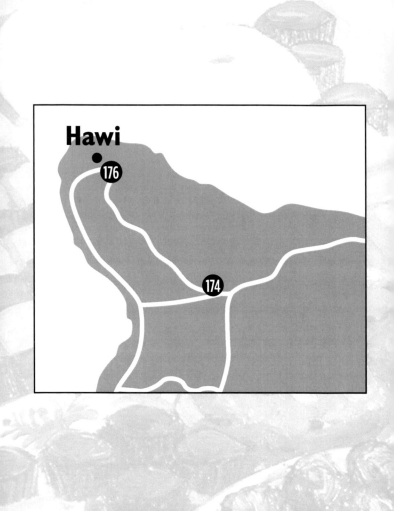

NORTH HAWAII

"We learned about the business through our parents, grandparents and numerous chefs. Restaurants have been in our family for four generations. We like being self-employed and watching our customers enjoy their food. Our success comes from great food, generous portions, reasonable prices, and friendly and courteous service to all customers."

Guy and Gina Kaoo

Hawaiian Style Cafe

WHERE STAY?	65-1290 Kawaihae Road Kamuela, Hawaii 96743 Phone 885-4295
WHEN OPEN?	Monday - Saturday, 7 a.m. - 1:30 p.m. Sunday, 7 a.m. - Noon
GOTTA GRIND	Variety of omelettes, oxtail soup, tripe stew, Hawaiian plates, kalbi, Korean pork, country-fried chicken, pastrami and French dip sandwiches
SEATING	Counter seats, four-seater booths and tables that seat four to six people
PARKING	No sweat! Parking in the front and rear
INSIDE SCOOPS	Celebrities such as Sam Choy, Alan Wong, Terry Bradshaw, Adam West, Uncle George Naope, the Brothers Cazimero and Frank Delima have frequented the diner. Accepts cash only.
CATERING?	No
ESTABLISHED	1992
NOTES	

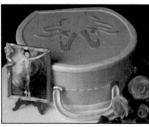

"I am a former pastry chef instructor for the merchant marines. I met my husband while I was teaching (he was a student). He was raised on the Big Island and we always knew we would return to Hawaii."

Maria Short

Short **N** Sweet
Bakery & Cafe

WHERE STAY? 55-3419 Akoni Pule Highway
Hawi, Hawaii 96719
Phone 889-1444

WHEN OPEN? Monday, Wednesday & Thursday,
9 a.m. - 6 p.m.
Friday - Saturday, 9 a.m. - 8:30 p.m.
Sunday, 9 a.m. - 2 p.m.

GOTTA GRIND Panini sandwiches on homemade
focaccia, pizza on homemade crust

GOTTA GRIND Spectacular homemade desserts
and pastries

SEATING Counter seating and 3 tables

PARKING No sweat! Parking in the rear of the
building and on the street

INSIDE SCOOPS This hole-in-the-wall showcases the
unique talents of a husband-and-wife
team. Maria is a culinary trained pastry
chef, while Dien learned about cooking
on cruise ships and as a merchant marine.
Dien is also a professional woodworker
and made all the furniture and doors for
the shop.

CATERING? Yes

ESTABLISHED 2006

NOTES

_____

_____

_____

_____

_____

_____

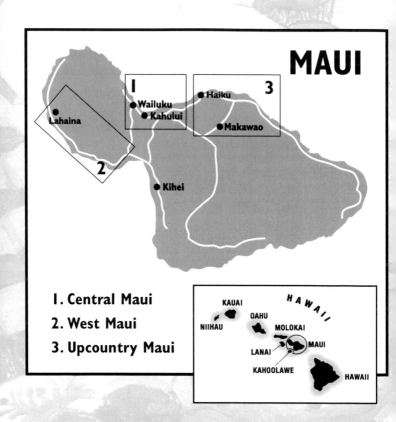

MAUI

1. Wailuku
   ● Kahului
   ● Haiku
3
● Lahaina
2
● Makawao
● Kihei

1. Central Maui
2. West Maui
3. Upcountry Maui

H A W A I I

KAUAI
NIIHAU
OAHU
MOLOKAI
LANAI
KAHOOLAWE
MAUI
HAWAII

MAUI

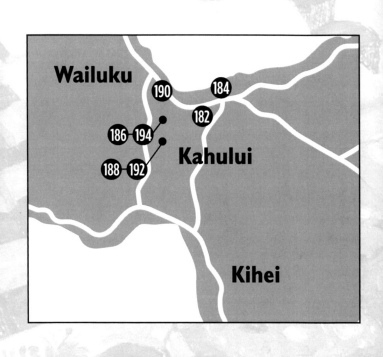

Central Maui

"*Good food at a good value always keeps customers coming back.*"

Lai Sei Cheung

Ajiyoshi Okazuya

WHERE STAY? 385 Hoohana Street., Ste. 5C
Kahului, Hawaii 96732-3512
Phone 877-9080

WHEN OPEN? Monday - Saturday, 10 a.m. - 2 p.m. and
4:30 p.m. - 8:30 p.m.
Sunday, closed

GOTTA GRIND Okazu: Oxtail soup, chicken katsu,
eggplant and the tempura plate

SEATING 10 tables, 36 seats

PARKING 12 stalls, plus street parking

INSIDE SCOOPS Accepts personal checks and credit cards.

CATERING? Yes

ESTABLISHED 1994

PUKA TRIVIA Customers from all over the world visit
Ajiyoshi Okazuya for its oxtail soup.
"The other day, a group of tourists from
Taiwan ordered our oxtail soup. They
had heard about us from a magazine
article written in Japanese. We didn't even
know about it," says Lai Sei Cheung.

NOTES _____

_____

_____

_____

_____

_____

_____

_____

_____

Da Kitchen

WHERE STAY?	425 Koloa Street, Ste. 104 Kahului, Hawaii 96732 Phone 871-7782 2439 South Kihei Road, Ste. A107 Kihei, Hawaii 96753 Phone 875-7782
WHEN OPEN?	Kahului location: Monday - Friday, 11 a.m. - 8 p.m. Saturday, 11 a.m. - 4 p.m. Sunday, closed Kihei location: Daily, 9 a.m. - 9 p.m.
GOTTA GRIND	Hawaiian plate, fish tempura, chicken katsu
SEATING	Booths and tables
PARKING	Parking lot
INSIDE SCOOPS	Accepts credit cards; no personal checks.
CATERING?	Yes
ESTABLISHED	Kihei location, 1998 Kahului location, 2000
PUKA TRIVIA	Restaurant owners wanted to close the Da Kitchen in 2001, but someone started a petition to keep it open and got approximately 2,000 signatures. TV station KHNL 8 once featured Da Kitchen on "Cheap Eats."
NOTES	_____ _____ _____ _____

"Ours is a family business, and I started as a youngster. My mother taught me how to prepare simple favorites and to cook by taste."

Jeremy Kozuki

Home Maid Bakery

Where Stay?	1005 Lower Main Street Wailuku, Hawaii 96793 Phone 244-4150
When Open?	Daily, 5 a.m. - 10 p.m.
Gotta Give	Crispy manju (azuki beans, apple, coconut, pineapple, peach, sweet potato, lima) and mochi (azuki beans, peanut butter), cookies
Besides Omiyage	Full line of bakery products, from dinner rolls to cakes
Seating	Take-out only!
Parking	No sweat! (18 stalls in a parking lot)
Inside Scoops	On holidays and for special orders, advance ordering is recommended. Accepts personal checks; no credit cards.
Catering?	No
Established	1960
Notes	

My dad was an only son, and he has four daughters, of which I'm the youngest. By carrying on Dad's business, we also carry on his name. Thus, people who don't know our family think that my husband, Charles Toma, is Sam Sato! We love seeing old-time customers who remember my parents and who feel nostalgic when they come here."

Lynne Toma

Sam Sato's

WHERE STAY?	1750 Wili Pa Loop Wailuku, Hawaii 96793 Phone 244-7124
WHEN OPEN?	Monday - Saturday, 7 a.m. - 2 p.m.
GOTTA GRIND	Dry noodles, saimin, manju and turnovers
SEATING	Seating for 50
PARKING	Parking lot and street parking
INSIDE SCOOPS	Traditionally closed for two and a half weeks in late September. Accepts personal checks.
CATERING?	No
ESTABLISHED	1933
PUKA TRIVIA	Restaurant owner Lynne Toma, who was a home economics major, learned how to cook from her mother. Lynne uses fresh ingredients and holds onto secret family recipes.
NOTES	

"Juikichi Tasaka started this business more than 90 years ago. My father Gunji Tasaka taught my younger brother, Setsuo, and I how to make Guri-Guri and operate the business. Ours is a unique product that is found only on Maui. Although there are a lot of imitations, people still come back to the original because the taste and quality can never be duplicated. This business has lasted four generations and hopefully will continue —if the fifth generation agrees to continue Tasaka's. This has been solely owned and operated by the Tasaka family and relatives."

Henry S. Tasaka

Tasaka Guri-Guri

Where Stay?	Maui Mall 70 East Kaahumanu Avenue Kahului, Hawaii 96732 Phone 871-4513
When Open?	Monday - Thursday, 10 a.m. - 6 p.m. Friday, 10 a.m. - 8 p.m. Saturday, 10 a.m. - 6 p.m. Sunday, 10 a.m. - 4 p.m.
Gotta Give	Guri-Guri sherbet (pineapple and strawberry)
Besides Omiyage	Hot dogs, drinks, chips
Seating	Take-out only!
Parking	No sweat! (Maui Mall parking lot)
Inside Scoops	Tasaka's Neighbor Island packs keep for 2-1/2 hours. Customers need to pick up no earlier than 1-1/2 hours before their flights. It is best to place these orders in advance.
Catering?	No
Established	Early 20th Century
Notes	

"We can safely say that we are a part of life on Maui. We are one of the last family-owned local restaurants."

Curis Takaoka

Tasty Crust

WHERE STAY?	1770 Mill Street Wailuku, Hawaii 96793 Phone 244-0845
WHEN OPEN?	Monday, 6 a.m. - 3 p.m. Tuesday - Thursday, 6 a.m. - 10 p.m. Friday - Saturday, 6 a.m. - 11 p.m.
GOTTA GRIND	Hotcakes, spare ribs and saimin
SEATING	Four long tables and 12 booths
PARKING	44 parking stalls on property
INSIDE SCOOPS	Cash only
CATERING?	No
ESTABLISHED	1944
PUKA TRIVIA	Curtis Takaoka's parents bought the store in 1957 and sold it in 1982. The family bought back the business in 1997. Although the store started as a bakery and evolved into a restaurant, staff members don't do any baking on-site. People come from all over just to sample the breakfast menu items.
NOTES	

"My mother always told me to clean up as you go, and that consistency was key, so that customers will always know that they are going to get what they expect."

Eunice Kitagawa
(granddaughter of restaurant founder, Kyutaro Kitagawa)

Tokyo Tei Restaurant

WHERE STAY?   1063 East Lower Main Street, Ste. C101
Wailuku, Hawaii 96793
Phone 242-9630

WHEN OPEN?   Tuesday - Saturday, 11 a.m. - 1:30 p.m.,
and 5 p.m. - 8:30 p.m.
Sunday, 5 p.m. - 8 p.m.
Monday, closed

GOTTA GRIND   Shrimp tempura and teriyaki steak

SEATING   Two and four tabletops that can be put
together for larger groups

PARKING   Parking in front of restaurant

INSIDE SCOOPS   Accepts credit cards; no personal checks.

CATERING?   Yes

ESTABLISHED   1934

PUKA TRIVIA   Kyutaro Kitagawa, a former sumo
wrestler in Japan, opened Tokyo Tei
restaurant in 1935 to support his
family. He had to change the name of
the restaurant to "Rainbow Grill" during
World War II.

NOTES   _____

_____

_____

_____

_____

_____

_____

_____

_____

_____

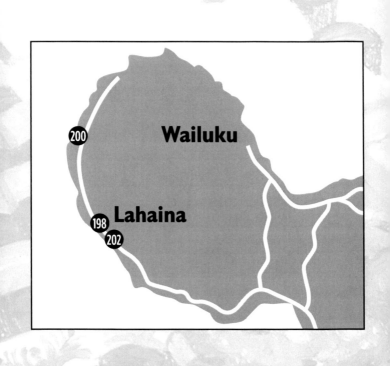

WEST MAUI

"The secret to our success is consistent quality and value, served with genuine aloha in a friendly, relaxing, oceanfront setting."

Julie Vigue

Aloha Mixed Plate

WHERE STAY?	1285 Front Street Lahaina, Hawaii 96761 Phone 661-3322
WHEN OPEN?	Daily, 10:30 a.m. - 10 p.m.
GOTTA GRIND	Kalua pig, kalbi ribs, coconut prawns, lau lau, chow fun, shoyu chicken
SEATING	Make house! (can seat up to 130 guests at 36 tables)
PARKING	No sweat! (20 stalls available, plus street parking)
INSIDE SCOOPS	*The New York Times* recently reviewed Aloha Mixed Plate. The editor wrote, "If you're looking for really good local food, Aloha Mixed Plate is the place to go. Just off Front Street and on the water's edge, Aloha Mixed Plate is a wonderful spot to grab a casual lunch or dinner." Accepts credit cards; no personal checks.
CATERING?	Yes
ESTABLISHED	1997
NOTES	_____ _____ _____ _____ _____ _____ _____ _____ _____ _____

Honokowai Okazuya

WHERE STAY?	3600 D. Lower Honoapiilani Road Lahaina, Hawaii 96761 Phone 665-0512
WHEN OPEN?	Monday - Saturday, 10 a.m. - 9 p.m.
GOTTA GRIND	Okazu: Lemon caper mahimahi, teriyaki steak
SEATING	2 tables outside, counter seating inside
PARKING	No sweat! Approximately 25 stalls
INSIDE SCOOPS	Cash only
CATERING?	Yes
ESTABLISHED	1997
NOTES	

"Our deli grew out of our fruit export business. We had pineapple, papaya and bananas that we used to make smoothies. The business grew from there. We model it after what we like in eating out—a healthy alternative to resort restaurant food. Most of our employees have been with us for more than 20 years, including Kehau, our African grey parrot. He sits on the lanai, whistles at all the bikini-clad girls or uses the colorful phrases learned from all the boat captains."

Raymond & Vickie Kadotani

Take Home Maui

WHERE STAY?	121 Dickenson Street Lahaina, Hawaii 96761 Phone 661-6185
WHEN OPEN?	Open daily, 6:30 a.m. - 7:30 p.m.
GOTTA GRIND	Deli sandwiches, loaded with fresh, fresh, fresh veggies
GOTTA GIVE	Gift baskets, Kona Coffee, Maui Gold low-acid pineapple and sweet Maui onions
SEATING	Lanai seating area overlooking Dickenson St.
PARKING	6 parking stalls in rear of building, plus paid parking lot across the street
INSIDE SCOOPS	Accepts personal checks and credit cards.
CATERING?	Yes
ESTABLISHED	1978
NOTES	

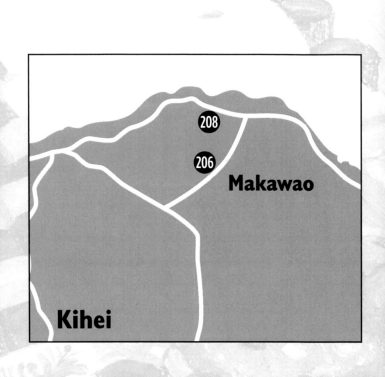

Upcountry Maui

"We're one of two original businesses that still exist in Makawao. We started out as a general story and our bakery product was very limited. One of the Komoda brothers went to baking school and began making pastries. And he still works here today."

Calvin Shibuya

Komoda Store & Bakery

WHERE STAY? 3674 Baldwin Avenue
Makawao, Hawaii 96768
Phone 572-7261
(corner of Baldwin & Makawao Avenues)

WHEN OPEN? Monday - Tuesday, 7 a.m. - 5 p.m.
Wednesday, closed
Thursday - Friday, 7 a.m. - 5 p.m.
Saturday, 7 a.m. - 2 p.m.
Sunday, closed

GOTTA GIVE Cream puffs, donuts, Long John, an pan
(baked and fried), azuki bean pie, cookies
(macadamia nut, chocolate chip, Rice
Krispies, short bread, peanut butter)

BESIDES OMIYAGE Full-service bakery; also some canned and
dry goods

SEATING Keep your eyes open! (3 tables)

PARKING Happy hunting! (small parking lot)

INSIDE SCOOPS For interisland or Mainland travel, preorder items at least one day in advance.
On busy days like Saturdays, Komoda
runs out of pastries by lunchtime, so get
there early! Accepts personal checks; no
credit cards.

CATERING? No

ESTABLISHED 1916

NOTES

208

"We're the last restaurant on the way to Hana. It's a great place to have a cup of coffee and relax. We like being out here in the country. We try to keep the spirit of aloha alive."

Brandon Shim

Pauwela Cafe

WHERE STAY? 375 West Kuiaha Road
Haiku, Hawaii 96708
Phone 575-9242

WHEN OPEN? Monday - Saturday, 7 a.m. - 2:30 p.m.
Sunday, 7 a.m. - 1 p.m.

GOTTA GRIND Health-conscience sandwiches and
smoothies. Fresh, homemade breads,
pastries and muffins, with European-style
coffee

SEATING Available seating

PARKING No sweat!

INSIDE SCOOPS Owner Brandon Shim, who recently
bought the cafe from one of his culinary
professors, has also worked at Tommy
Bahama's Tropical Café & Emporium and
Hailiimaile General Store. He bakes all
the breads and pastries. Accepts local
personal checks and credit cards.

CATERING? Yes

ESTABLISHED 1992

NOTES

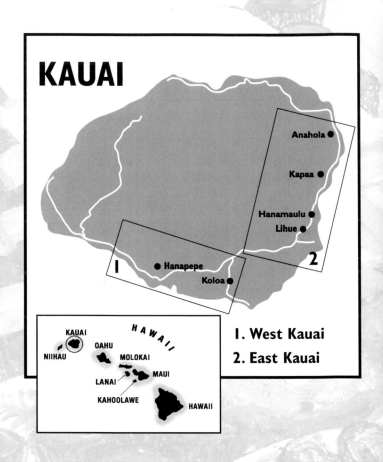

KAUAI

Anahola ●

Kapaa ●

Hanamaulu ●
Lihue ●

2

1

● Hanapepe

Koloa ●

KAUAI
NIIHAU
OAHU
MOLOKAI
LANAI
KAHOOLAWE
MAUI
HAWAII
HAWAII

1. West Kauai
2. East Kauai

KAUAI

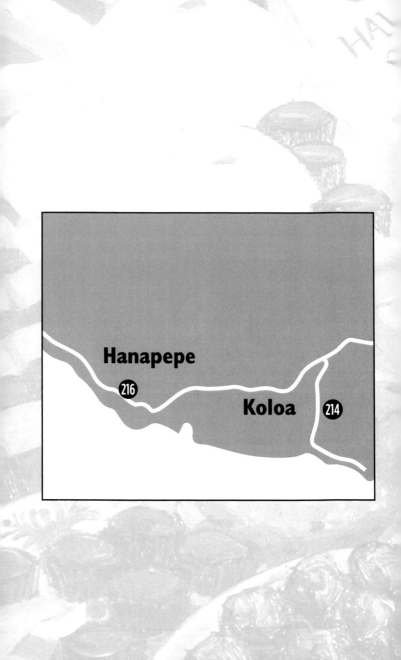

West Kauai

"I always wanted to start my own business!"

Bert Matsuoka

Koloa Fish Market

WHERE STAY?	5482 Koloa Road Koloa, Hawaii 96756 Phone 742-6199
WHEN OPEN?	Monday - Friday, 10 a.m. - 6 p.m. Saturday, 10 a.m. - 5 p.m. Sunday, closed
GOTTA GRIND	Hawaiian plate lunch and daily specials
SEATING	Take-out only
PARKING	Street parking
INSIDE SCOOPS	Cash only
CATERING?	Yes
ESTABLISHED	1994
PUKA TRIVIA	Owner Bert Matsuoka was executive chef at the Sheraton Kauai Hotel before Hurricane Iniki destroyed the property and left him without a job. The disaster motivated him to start his own business.
NOTES	

"We get a lot of tourists who come to buy our pies. For instance, every year a lady from Texas stops by. She even sends us cards and small gifts, and she always says how nice my mom is. Everyone loved my dad, too—the way he used to play jokes on the customers. Everyone remembers his famous saying: 'Eat at Wong's, you can't go wrong!'"

Julia Wong

Wong's Restaurant & Omoide Deli

WHERE STAY? 13543 Kaumualii Highway
Hanapepe, Hawaii 96716
Phone 335-5066

WHEN OPEN? Monday, closed
Tuesday - Sunday, 9:30 a.m. - 9 p.m.

GOTTA GIVE Famous pies (lilikoi chiffon, macadamia nut cream, banana cream), square cream puffs

BESIDES OMIYAGE Hamburgers and plate lunches (Chinese, Filipino and other local food)

SEATING Make house! (seats up to 300 people)

PARKING No sweat! (parking lot and parking stalls around the building)

INSIDE SCOOPS They always have a supply of frozen pies packed and ready to take on the airplane. Call in advance for cream puffs so your order can be packed for travel. Usually closed for vacation for two weeks in September. Accepts local checks (no out-of-state) and credit cards.

CATERING? Yes

ESTABLISHED 1982

NOTES

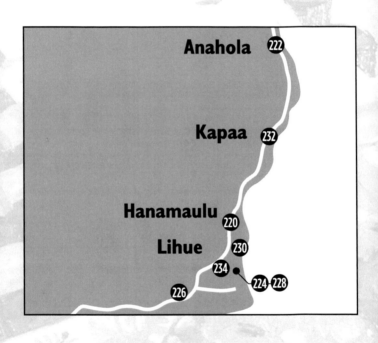

EAST KAUAI

"Our family has been in the restaurant business for more than 80 years. I enjoy pleasing our customers. The secret to our success is hard work. Plus, we constantly change what we sell and bring in different items."

Debra Aramaki

Ara's Sakana-Ya

WHERE STAY?   3-4301 Kuhio Highway, Ste. 102
Hanamaulu, Hawaii 96715
Phone 245-1707

WHEN OPEN?   Monday - Saturday, 10 a.m. - 6 p.m.
Sunday, 9 a.m. - 2 p.m.

GOTTA GRIND   Cheap beer, pupu, sashimi and
sushi platters

SEATING   Take-out only

PARKING   No sweat! (parking at Hanamaulu Plaza
Shopping Center)

INSIDE SCOOPS   Locals come for lunch for the variety
of food, quick turnaround times and
affordable prices. Accepts credit cards,
but no personal checks.

CATERING?   Sushi, pupu and sashimi platters

ESTABLISHED   1986

NOTES

Duane's Ono Char Burger

WHERE STAY? 4-4350 Kuhio Highway
Anahola, Hawaii 96703
Phone 822-9181

WHEN OPEN? Monday - Saturday, 10 a.m. - 6 p.m.
Sunday, 11 a.m. - 6 p.m.

GOTTA GRIND Local Boy (teriyaki, cheddar cheese
and pineapple)

SEATING 3 round tables seating 6,
5 square tables seating 4,
3 picnic tables seating 6

PARKING No sweat! (parking lot on site)

INSIDE SCOOPS Accepts personal checks and credit cards.

CATERING? No

ESTABLISHED 1975

NOTES

"Hamura's is a family operation that got passed down. Our grandparents, the original owners, taught us about the business and how to cook. We enjoy serving our customers well and they are very satisfied with what we serve."

Laurel Tanigawa

Hamura's Saimin

WHERE STAY?
2956 Kress Street
Lihue, Hawaii 96766
Phone 245-3271

WHEN OPEN?
Monday - Thursday, 10 a.m. - 10:30 p.m.
Friday - Saturday, 10 a.m. - Midnight
Sunday, 10 a.m. - 9:30 p.m.

GOTTA GRIND
The teriyaki barbecue sticks and
steaming saimin bowls, heaped with
dense noodles, full-bodied broth,
vegetables, wontons, hard-boiled eggs,
sweetened pork, vegetables and
condiments, attract an all-day crowd.

GOTTA GIVE
Lilikoi chiffon pie, which can be packed
for interisland travel

SEATING
Make house!

PARKING
No sweat! (space for at least 10 cars)

INSIDE SCOOPS
In 2006, Hamura's won an "America's
Classics" James Beard Award. Closed one
week after Labor Day in September.
Accepts cash only.

CATERING?
No

ESTABLISHED
1950

NOTES

_____

_____

_____

_____

_____

_____

_____

_____

_____

"I'm actually a full-time firefighter. I started baking as a hobby, making sweetbread. I used to cook at a restaurant in Lihue and got bored, so I tried baking. But everything I know, I learned through trial and error."

David Taboniar

Hanalima Baking

WHERE STAY?	4495 Puhi Road Lihue, Hawaii 96766 Phone 246-8816
WHEN OPEN?	Monday - Friday, 6 a.m. - 12:30 p.m. Saturday, 7 a.m. - 12:30 p.m. Sunday, closed
GOTTA GIVE	Butter cookies (also guava, furikake, chocolate), crab rolls, breads (sweet bread and Italian-style)
BESIDES OMIYAGE	Try the sandwiches and wraps, they're ono.
SEATING	Take-out only! (some chairs outside)
PARKING	No sweat! (parking lot)
INSIDE SCOOPS	Call in advance and Hanalima will pack items for airplane travel.
CATERING?	No, but the bakery will cut pastries in half for large group orders. Accepts personal checks and credit cards.
ESTABLISHED	1997 (at current location since 2000)
NOTES	

Lihue Barbeque Inn, Ltd.

WHERE STAY?
2982 Kress Street
Lihue, Hawaii 96766
Phone 245-2921

WHEN OPEN?
Breakfast:
Monday - Saturday, 7 a.m. - 10:30 a.m.
Lunch:
Monday - Saturday, 10:30 a.m. - 1:30 p.m.
Dinner:
Monday - Thursday, 5 p.m - 8:30 p.m.
Friday - Saturday, 4:30 p.m. - 8:45 p.m.

GOTTA GRIND
Majority of the items on the menu come as a complete meal. Homemade bread, soup, salad and cream pie

SEATING
4-seater booths and tables

PARKING
Limited parking

INSIDE SCOOPS
Accepts credit cards

CATERING?
No

ESTABLISHED
1940

NOTES

_____

_____

_____

_____

_____

_____

_____

_____

_____

_____

"The success of my business comes from the employees, not the employer!"

Poh Yamamoto

Po's Kitchen

WHERE STAY?	4100 Rice Street Lihue, Hawaii 96766 Phone 246-8617
WHEN OPEN?	Daily, 6 a.m. - 2 p.m.
GOTTA GRIND	Okazu: Cone sushi and box lunches
PARKING	Parking lot
INSIDE SCOOPS	Cash only
CATERING?	Yes
ESTABLISHED	1993
PUKA TRIVIA	In the early 1990s, owner Poh Yamamoto owned a gift and jewelry business, which tanked after Hurricane Iniki caused Kauai's tourism industry to hit rock bottom. Noting a construction boom on the island after the hurricane, Yamamoto decided to open a food business. It has been at its existing location for the past 10 years. "I'm originally from Malaysia, where hot, spicy foods were my favorite. I took quite a bit of lessons whenever I went back to Malaysia," says Yamamoto.
NOTES	

"The secret to our success? The love and aloha we have for everyone—both workers and customers. We've seen them grow up from preschool to being parents of their own."

Bob and Lynn Kubota

Pono Market

WHERE STAY?
4-1300 Kuhio Highway
Kapaa, Hawaii 96746
Phone 822-4581

WHEN OPEN?
Monday - Friday, 6 a.m. - 6 p.m.
Saturday, 6 a.m. - 4 p.m.
Sunday, closed

GOTTA GRIND
Okazu: Lau lau, poke, sushi, fried chicken, roast pork, potato-macaroni salad, stuff chicken and manju

SEATING
No seating

PARKING
Street parking

INSIDE SCOOPS
Cash and Kauai personal checks only

CATERING?
No

ESTABLISHED
1968

PUKA TRIVIA
Minoru Kubota started the business in 1968, and his wife, Kiyoko, with only an eighth-grade education, made sure that all of the bills were paid. Today, Pono Market is owned by Bob Kubota and his wife, Lynn, who cooks and manages the kitchen. She learned how to cook from Kiyoko and her own mother, Ellen Sugita. Brother Kenneth operates an espresso bar within the market, named Mino's Coffee & Tea, named after his dad, who liked to drink coffee.

NOTES
_____

_____

_____

_____

_____

Sushi Katsu

WHERE STAY?	3173 Akahi Street Lihue, HI 96766 Phone 246-0176
WHEN OPEN?	Tuesday - Sunday, 11 a.m. - 2 p.m. Monday, closed
GOTTA GRIND	Okazu: Deluxe set, with fresh local fish, nigiri and rolls
SEATING	20 tables, sushi bar (seats 60-70 people)
PARKING	No sweat! (plenty parking in front and sides of restaurant)
INSIDE SCOOPS	Closed on Thanksgiving, Christmas, New Year's Eve, New Year's Day and the day after. Accepts credit cards.
CATERING?	No
ESTABLISHED	1996
NOTES	

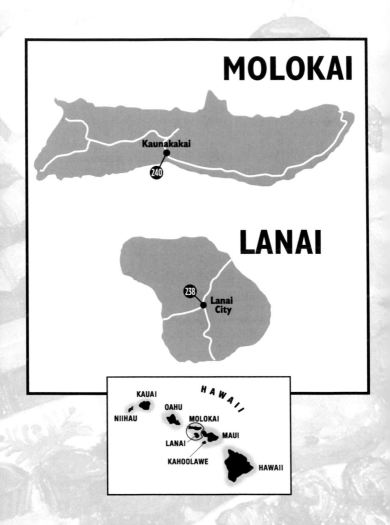

Lanai & Molokai

237

"What's most enjoyable for us is working with our employees and getting to meet and know our wonderful customers."

Joseph & Georgia Abilay

Blue Ginger Cafe

WHERE STAY?   409 7th Street
Lanai City, Hawaii 96763
Phone 565-6363

WHEN OPEN?   Daily, 6 a.m. - 8 p.m.

GOTTA GIVE   Apple turnovers, fresh-baked bread, a
variety of "Blue Ginger Cafe" T-shirts

BESIDES OMIYAGE   Plate lunches, including fried saimin,
chop steak and hamburgers

SEATING   Make house! (12 tables, 46 chairs)

PARKING   No sweat!

CATERING?   Yes

ESTABLISHED   1991

INSIDE SCOOP   Accept personal checks; no credit cards.

CATERING?   Yes

NOTES   _____

_____

_____

_____

_____

_____

_____

_____

_____

_____

_____

_____

"I enjoy seeing people come back to visit us. Sometimes they go back to the Mainland and write us a letter to tell us how much they enjoyed everything. And their friends come over because they were told that if they ever get to Molokai, they should come and see us."

George Kanemitsu

Kanemitsu Bakery & Restaurant

WHERE STAY?
79 Ala Malama Street
Kaunakakai, Hawaii 96748
Phone 553-5855

WHEN OPEN?
Bakery:
Monday, 5:30 a.m. - 6:30 p.m.
Tuesday, closed
Wednesday - Sunday, 5:30 a.m. - 6:30 p.m.

GOTTA GIVE
Molokai Bread, Molokai Bread mix (sesame, cinnamon, macadamia nut, onion and taro), cookies (macadamia nut, chocolate chip, oatmeal and shortbread)

BESIDES OMIYAGE
The restaurant serves hamburgers and breakfast. (Monday - Friday, 5:30 a.m. - Noon; Saturday - Saturday, 5:30 a.m. - 12:30 p.m.)

SEATING
Make house! (14 tables)

PARKING
No sweat! (street parking)

INSIDE SCOOPS
Call one day in advance to ensure availability of items. Accepts personal checks and credit cards.

CATERING?
Yes

ESTABLISHED
1935

NOTES

GLOSSARY

adobo	Filipino dish of pork or chicken
andagi	Okinawan fried donut
anpan	Japanese roll filled with sweet bean paste (also an pan)
arare	Japanese rice cracker, also called mochi crunch
azuki	sweet bean paste made with Japanese red beans
char siu	red, sweet barbecued pork, usually colored red on the outside pork
chichi dango	soft, sweet, milky glutinous rice cake dusted with mochiko (glutinous rice flour) or kinako
chiso	leaf of the beefsteak plant
cracked seed	Chinese dried fruits, usually plums preserved in a sauce of five-spice, sugar and salt
dashi	Japanese fish stock
furikake	roasted seaweed, salt, sesame seeds often sprinkled on rice
guisantes	Filipino dish; meat or poultry cooked with peppers and peas in a tomato sauce base
habutai mochi	poofy-domed rice cake filled with sweet azuki and dusted with kinako
haupia	coconut pudding
hekka	meat, translucent noodles, bamboo shoots and mushrooms simmered in a shoyu-based sauce
inari sushi	more commonly known as cone sushi; sweet vinegar-flavored rice placed inside fried tofu
kabocha	pumpkin simmered in a sauce
kal bi	Korean barbecued short ribs with teriyaki marinade
kanpyo	dried gourd strips
katsu	breaded pork or chicken cutlet
kim chee	Korean appetizer; hot, salty pickled cabbage
kinako	soy flour
kinpira gobo	burdock (root) sliced thin and simmered
kobu (konbu)	dried kelp
kobu maki	chicken or pork wrapped in kobu, tied with kanpyo
koko	Hawaii slang for Japanese takuan (pickled vegetables, including turnip, radish and cucumber)
lau lau	salted pork, beef or fish and/or taro tops, wrapped in ti leaves and baked or steamed
lechon kawali	Filipino dish; crispy roasted pork
lilikoi	tart fruit, also called passion fruit
limu	seaweed
loco moco	a dish of rice, hamburger patty and an over-easy egg, all covered with brown gravy (originated on the Big Island)
lomi salmon	cold salad made with chopped salted salmon, diced tomatoes and onions
luau stew	beef with taro leaf
lumpia	Filipino spring roll; vegetables and ground pork in a thin rice wrapper and deep fried
lup cheong	Chinese sausage

ma tai su	baked dumplings, often filled with char siu and chopped water chestnuts
maki sushi	sweet vinegar-flavored rice rolled in nori; sometimes includes items such as egg, kanpyo, carrots and tuna flakes
malassadas	Portuguese fried donut coated with sugar
manapua	Chinese-style buns, steamed or baked and filled with vegetable and meat
manju	baked flaky pastries filled with sweetened pastes including azuki bean and sweet potato
meat jun	Korean dish; barbecue meat dipped in egg batter and fried
miso	fermented soybean paste
misoyaki	fish marinated in miso, then grilled
mochi	Japanese steamed cake made with sweet rice flour (mochiko), often filled with azuki beans
mochi crunch	Japanese rice cracker, also called arare
mochiko	sweet rice flour
musubi	rice ball sometimes wrapped with a strip of nori and filled with ume
naau luau	pig intestines with taro leaf
nishime	vegetable stew; includes items such as kobu, carrots, lotus root, bamboo shoots and tofu
nori	dried seaweed used to wrap sushi
okoshi	sweet puffed rice cake
oyako donburi	chicken and egg on rice
pastele	Puerto Rican dish; mashed green banana and spiced pork
pipikaula	sun-dried salted beef, sliced thin as a snack
poi	steamed taro mashed with a little water
poke	marinated raw fish
pupu	appetizer
saba	mackerel
saimin	noodle soup with broth made with dashi and thin, round wheat noodles; often garnished with scrambled eggs or omelet, meats, green onions, kamaboko, char siu
sashimi	raw meat (usually fish)
senbei	Japanese tea cookie
tako	octopus
teishoku	set meal; special of the day
tempura	shrimp, sweet potato or vegetables battered and deep-fried
udon	thick wheat noodles
ume	salty picked plum; usually placed in the middle of a musubi
wakame	Japanese seaweed
yakisoba	fried noodles
yakitori	barbecued or grilled meat on a bamboo skewer

INDEX BY NAME

INDEX BY LOCATION

Oahu

HONOLULU

CENTRAL / LEEWARD OAHU

ABOUT THE AUTHORS

Donovan M. Dela Cruz and Jodi Endo Chai were both born and raised in the central Oahu town of Wahiawa and—like Foreword contributor Alan Wong— graduated from Leilehua High School.

A Honolulu City Council member since 2003, Donovan represents Council District 2, which encompasses Miliani Mauka, Wahiawa, North Shore, Koolauloa and part of Kaneohe. Prior to entering public service, Donovan worked in the public relations field at two of Hawaii's top PR agencies. He is active in community affairs and enjoys being involved in community groups such as the Wahiawa Lions. Writing *The Puka Guide* series enables Donovan to pursue his passion for preserving local culture and promoting local restaurants and businesses. He believes that the road to a great eatery is never long.

Besides being a wife and mother, Jodi is the Communications Officer for Hawaii's largest public employee union, the Hawaii Government Employees Association. Her love for nostalgic eateries stems from her formative years in Wahiawa—when she ate Sunnyside pies at family dinners and snacked on Kilani Bakery brownies with friends at sleepovers, and when one of the highlights of elementary school field trips was eating her bento from the neighborhood okazuya. Today, she says, Hawaii's hole-in-the-wall restaurants evoke that earlier, simpler era in Island culture.